noted chirped
ated blabbed
bleated jabbered
d commented
ed confessed
stormed rebuked
cast howled
arled blathered
ated nagged
choed prattled
med heeled

In Other Words

A BEGINNING THESAURUS

W. Cabell Greet

William A. Jenkins

Andrew Schiller

In Other Words

Contents

What Is a Synonym?

"A synonym is a word that has about the same meaning as another word," Joe said.

"It's a word that means almost the same as another word," exclaimed Susie.

"A word with approximately the same meaning," Judy stated firmly.

"It's nearly the same, and it can be used instead of that word," Bill added.

"Practically the same!" agreed Jack.

Jerry thought for a moment before he spoke. "Could you say it is virtually the same?" he suggested.

"How about calling it well-nigh the same?" shouted Tom. He always liked to show off.

Who was right? All of the boys and girls, of course. And as they told what a synonym is, each one used a synonym.

In other words, *about, almost, approximately, practically, nearly, virtually,* and *well-nigh* were all good words for the children to use when answering the question.

As you read the answers, perhaps you noticed another interesting thing. Each child said something. But Susie *exclaimed.* Judy *stated.* Bill *added.* Jack *agreed.* Jerry *suggested.* Tom *shouted.* Can't you see how excited and interested these children were? If each one had just *said* something, would you have noticed that they were eager to talk about synonyms?

Perhaps words like *shouted, agreed,* and *added* don't really mean almost the same as *said,* but they do show exactly how Bill and Jack and Tom spoke.

Bill went on. "I know where to find synonyms, too. My dad has about a million of them."

"A million of them!" Jack echoed Bill's words.

"Where?" demanded Judy.

Bill smiled. "In a thesaurus."

"A *what?*" Tom shouted.

"A the- the- huh?" stuttered Joe.

Judy and Susie stared at Bill with their mouths open. They were speechless.

What Is a Thesaurus?

A thesaurus is a treasury—and a treasury is a place where valuable things are kept. This book is a thesaurus—a treasury of words—and words are valuable. Here you can find the very words you need for whatever you are telling about or whatever you want to write about.

The first part of this book tells you how to use it. You will learn how to look up words, how to find synonyms and antonyms, and how to pick out the best synonyms to use.

The second part lists all the words, synonyms, and antonyms in alphabetical order.

The third part contains sets of pictured objects, people, and animals.

1

How to Use This Book

About This Book . . . Things to Know

You may think a thesaurus is some kind of dictionary—until you take a good look at it. It has entry words. So does a dictionary. It has them listed alphabetically. So does a dictionary. In a dictionary you can find every word you have ever heard of—and hundreds of words you have *never* heard of. You can learn what the words mean and how they should be pronounced.

But this thesaurus has only one hundred entry words, and you probably know them!

WORN-OUT WORDS

Most of these entry words are used so often and are used for saying so many different things that they are practically worn out. The whole purpose of this book is to give you some other words to use.

These other words are used as synonyms or antonyms of the one hundred entry words. You can find any word—if it is in the book—by looking it up alphabetically. If it is not an entry word, it will be listed with a sentence that tells you in which entry you will find it. Words listed this way are called *cross references*.

Here is an example of what you will find in an entry. (But you won't find this entry in the book.)

An entry contains an entry word	HIGH
an explanation of how it is used	HIGH is the opposite of low. It means being above or reaching above other objects nearby. You speak of a *high* hill or a *high* shelf.
synonyms	*tall* *lofty* *towering*
explanations and sample sentences or phrases	*Tall* describes something grown or made to extend far above the ground. A *tall* building is a skyscraper. A low building is not. *Lofty* means very high in position. You might call mountain peaks *lofty* with deep valleys between them. *Towering* describes something high and rising over nearby objects. *We were surrounded by towering trees.*
antonyms	low short deep

Cross references look like this:

DEEP   Look up antonyms of HIGH.
LOFTY   Look up HIGH.

There is one other kind of word listed in this book. If a verb has an irregular past tense (-*ed* form) and past participle (-*en* form) these forms are listed. Here is a sample:

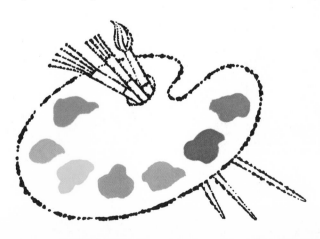

FLEW   FLEW is the past tense of FLY.
FLOWN   FLOWN is the past participle of FLY.

An entry in this thesaurus will show you the shades of difference in meaning between synonyms, and it will help you select the best ones for whatever use you have in mind. It will also offer you some precise words that you can use to say exactly what you mean. It can help you use those words as skillfully as an artist uses colors when he paints a picture.

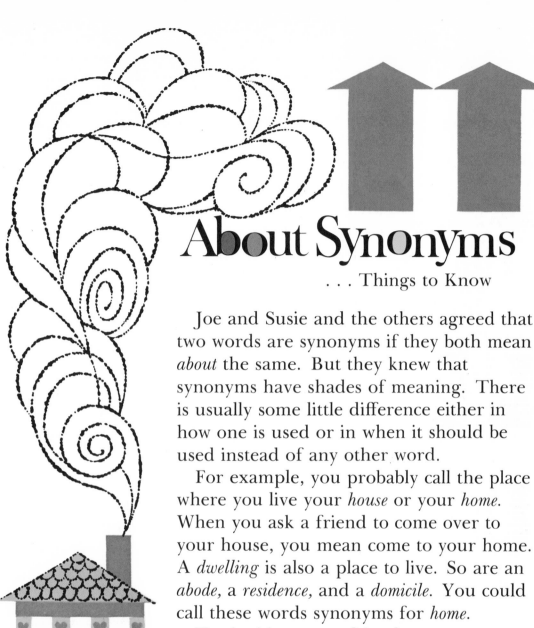

About Synonyms

. . . Things to Know

Joe and Susie and the others agreed that two words are synonyms if they both mean *about* the same. But they knew that synonyms have shades of meaning. There is usually some little difference either in how one is used or in when it should be used instead of any other word.

For example, you probably call the place where you live your *house* or your *home.* When you ask a friend to come over to your house, you mean come to your home. A *dwelling* is also a place to live. So are an *abode,* a *residence,* and a *domicile.* You could call these words synonyms for *home.*

Try inviting some friends to a party at your domicile. Or tell your mother you are going across the street to your friend's abode. You will probably get some surprised looks, but what you said is perfectly correct.

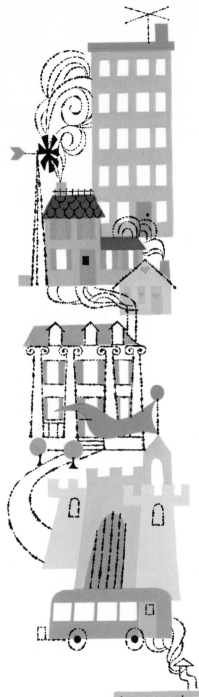

When you begin to use or think of some other words for *house*, though, be careful!

The place where you live might be an apartment or a flat or a farmhouse. It might be a cottage or a mansion or a castle or a trailer or a houseboat. Suppose you invited some friends to a party at your cottage, and when they arrived at the address you gave them, they saw a twenty-story apartment building. They would probably go right on by. They'd probably never get to your party. What would your teacher think if you told her you lived in the trailer between the castle and the houseboat on top of the hill?

You can't use one of these words in place of another and mean the same thing, any more than you can call a river a lake, even though both are places where fish live. A cottage, mansion, trailer, and the rest do have something in common, though. They are all places in which people live. So they could be called a *set* of dwellings.

Sets of things that have something in common—sets of people and objects and animals—are pictured in the last section of this book.

About Antonyms

... Things to Know

An antonym is a word that means the opposite of another word. *Up* is the antonym, or opposite, of *down*. *Inside* is the antonym, or opposite, of *outside*. Sometimes a quick way to find out what a word means is to find out what it does not mean. What could be quicker than this, for example:

Keep Out means "Don't Come In!" If you know what *happy* means, you'll have a pretty good idea of the meaning of *unhappy*.

But some antonyms can be tricky, too. *Up* and *down* are easy. You can't be up and down at the same time. (Well, if you are halfway up a hill, you are *up* to the people who are at the bottom, and *down* to the people who are at the top, of course.) *Inside* and *outside* are easy, too. You can't be inside and outside at the same time. (Oh, you could stand in the middle of the doorway and be half inside and half outside. If you did, though, somebody would probably shout at you to shut the door.) But it is simple to see that these four antonyms, *up* and *down, inside* and *outside,* are truly opposites.

13

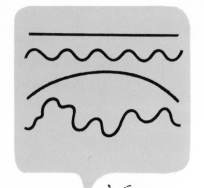

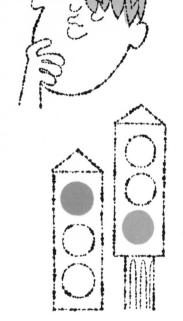

Now, think of a straight line. ——————
Crooked means not straight.   But look what happens when you try to think of a crooked line. You might think
or
or
or any kind of crazy-looking line. The first crooked line could be called *wavy.* The second is *curved.* The third may be called *meandering*—because it wanders all around. So here are three words that can be synonyms of *crooked* and antonyms of *straight,* even though their meanings are different from each other.

Which crooked word would you use to describe a brook?

What's the opposite of *go? Stop,* of course —but how about *come?* The opposite of *right* is *left*—and *wrong.* A word like *right* can have more than one antonym, or opposite. A word like *right* can be the antonym of two words that have quite different meanings.

About Entries

. . . Things to Know

Look up the word *friend.* You'll see that it is an entry word, printed in capitals out in

14

the left-hand margin of the page. Beside the entry word is a paragraph that tells what a friend is (as if you didn't already know).

In the margin below the entry six synonyms are listed. These are **printed in black, heavy type.** Each of these synonyms is described in the text. One of the synonyms, **companion,** is used in a sentence. Wherever an entry word or a synonym or antonym is used in a sample sentence, you will find the sentence *printed in italic type.*

At the end of the entry are antonyms for *friend.* Antonyms are printed in regular type, but they are easy to find and recognize because they are always underlined in blue.

TIRED WORDS

There are a few entries in this book that do not have any synonyms listed in the margin. CUTE and NICE are two of them. These words are so tired and overworked that they deserve a good, long rest. Look them up and see what to use instead.

TWO-WAY WORDS

If you see the letters (n), (v), (adj), or (adv) after an entry word, you will know that that word can be used in more ways than it is used in the entry. The abbreviation

(n) means *noun;* (v) means *verb;* (adj) means *adjective;* (adv) means *adverb.*

Look up ANSWER (n) and ANSWER (v). After reading both these entries, turn to the R's and look at RESPOND and RESPONSE. You can tell which word is a synonym for ANSWER (v) and which for ANSWER (n). Now look at RETORT. That is a synonym for both the noun and the verb *answer.*

Look up SLOWLY and see if you can tell why you were referred to FAST (adv) instead of to just FAST.

Some synonyms are followed, in a sentence, by another word in the same black type. Look up LOVE. You will see that **affection for** and **devotion to** are all in the same type. At the end of the entry is a sentence telling when to use **for** and when to use **to.**

More ... Things to Know

Some entries contain special information that other entries do not have. Look at the explanation for the synonym **comrade,** in the entry FRIEND. This word has traveled far in history, and you may be interested to know where it went and how it changed.

When an entry is a verb that has an irregular past tense and past participle, both forms appear in sentences. Look at the entry SHUT, for examples of how to use these forms.

Not every entry has antonyms listed, because not every word has an antonym. Take *dive,* for example. It simply has no opposite. Neither has *guess.* Can you think of an opposite for *peel* or *sneeze* or *journey?* So don't be worried when you come across an entry without antonyms.

Many entries contain sentences at the end which tell you to look up other words. *Bright,* for example, is a word that can describe sunshine, but it can also describe an intelligent person. Look at the entry BRIGHT. At the end of it, you are directed to look also at synonyms in the entry SMART. The word *smart* and its synonyms do not really describe the same things *bright* describes. (You wouldn't call sunshine *smart* or *clever.*) So there is no sentence under SMART telling you to look up BRIGHT.

What synonym would you use to describe sunshine?

Break and *cut* mean different things. Some of the synonyms of one, however, could be used for the other. *Slit* could mean either cut or tear a piece of cloth. *Chip* could mean cut small pieces from a rock or

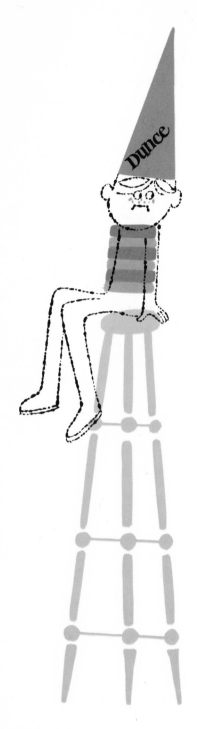

break a small piece from the edge of a dish. So a sentence in each entry—BREAK and CUT—tells you that in the other one you might find a word which could express more exactly what you want to say.

Sometimes a sentence in an entry tells you to look up antonyms of another word. Turn back to BRIGHT and notice that you are directed to see antonyms for DIM and STUPID. If you look up DIM and STUPID, you'll find some of the same words in both lists of antonyms, but you will also find some different ones.

There is one synonym for both DIM and STUPID that you might use to describe a day without any sunshine at all. See if you can find it.

In an entry a word listed as an antonym is not always the opposite of every synonym. Look up the entry HARD. The word *easy* is one of its antonyms. But how many synonyms would you say are the opposite of *easy*—three or four at the most? Nobody would use *easy* to mean "not solid" or "not rigid" or "not firm."

Sometimes an antonym is not even the opposite of the entry word. It might be the opposite of just one or two of the synonyms in that entry. QUIET (adj) is a good example. Look up the entry. One of the antonyms is *wild*. Look at the synonyms and find one

that means the opposite of *wild*. You will probably choose *tame*. A *tame* animal is not *wild*. You might also choose *calm* and *peaceful*. A "wild" ocean might be considered the opposite of a "calm" or "peaceful" ocean. But you would not use *wild* as the opposite of *speechless* or *dumb* or *numb*. When a word is an antonym of just one or two synonyms, a sentence in the entry tells you so. See the sentence in QUIET— *"Tame is the opposite of wild."*

Think of a sentence using the word *calm*. Could you use *speechless* instead of *calm* in that sentence? Could you use *dumb*?

About Choosing Synonyms

. . . Things to Know

You know that synonyms have different shades of meaning. So you also know that you will have to consider them quite carefully before choosing the one you want to use.

Suppose you had seen a very funny sight on the street one day and you wanted to describe it to a friend. If you look up FUNNY, you will find an entry with nine

synonyms. The synonym you use will depend on how you want to describe the funny sight.

For example, look at this hat. Some people might call it a funny-looking hat. (The lady who bought it certainly would not!) Suppose you had seen a tiny girl— about four years old—walking along the sidewalk, wearing this hat and a long dress and a pair of her mother's shoes. The first synonym listed under FUNNY is *amusing*. *Amusing* describes a story or a sight or anything that catches your attention in a pleasant way and makes you laugh. Do you think *amusing* would be a good word to describe this sight?

Suppose, though, that what you had seen was a horse, wearing this hat and pulling a wagon down the street. Which synonym would you choose to describe that sight? Several of them could do it, but probably *comical* could do it best. Can you see why?

What if you had seen that hat, on the lady who bought it, just after she had been caught in a sudden, terrible rain?

Perhaps you couldn't help laughing because she was a funny sight, but you would feel sorry for her, too. The best synonym to describe her would be *ludicrous*. Read the explanation of *ludicrous* and see if you agree.

20

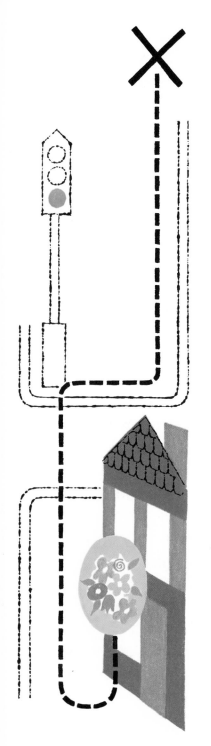

You will probably find some other long words like **ludicrous** in this book. Perhaps you have never heard them before. But you will find them good words to use. Just look in your dictionary for their pronunciations and definitions. Then see if their shades of meaning, as given in this book, make them appropriate for what you want to say.

Wait a minute, now. Suppose you had seen that hat coming down the street by itself! It was not being blown by the wind or rolling down the sidewalk. It was just moving along, about three feet above the ground. Suppose you watched it turn a corner, stop for a traffic light, then cross the street and move right up the side of a tall building!

You might call that a funny sight, but would you feel much like laughing? Or would you feel more like running away?

Funny is a word like *bright*. Besides describing something that makes you laugh, *funny* can describe something strange or weird—like a funny sound in a house that you know is empty.

At the end of the entry FUNNY you are told that the entry QUEER might suggest words which would express better what you want to say. Look up QUEER and see what you think.

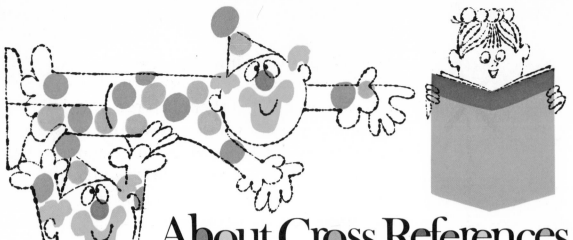

About Cross References
. . . Things to Know

When you read the last sentence in the entry FUNNY, you were told to look up QUEER. In other words, this sentence referred you to another entry. This is a cross reference. You have already seen examples of regular cross references. Just to make sure you remember, look one up. Take *comical,* one of the synonyms for FUNNY. Now look it up in the C's. Then try another one—*amusing.* What is different about the cross reference for *amusing?* You are right if you noticed that you are told to look up two entries instead of one. Look up INTERESTING and see how the word *amusing* may be used as a synonym for it. Can you think of a sentence, using *amusing* to mean "funny"? How about another sentence, using it to mean "interesting"?

As you write or tell about something you saw, you might want to use a different word

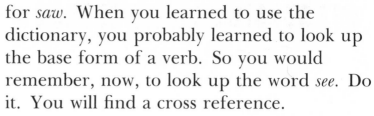

for *saw*. When you learned to use the dictionary, you probably learned to look up the base form of a verb. So you would remember, now, to look up the word *see*. Do it. You will find a cross reference.

If you should forget about finding the base form of the verb, it wouldn't matter. Look up *saw*. Remember what you read earlier about verbs with irregular forms? Here is a sentence to remind you that *see* is the word to look up. But notice that there is another cross reference for *saw*. How do you know that is not the one you want? If you are not sure, of course, you can look up both SEE and CUT. These words would probably not give you any trouble, but if you find two cross references somewhere and aren't quite sure which word you want, read both entries.

There is one other kind of cross reference. Look up EASY. You will find that it refers you only to the antonyms of HARD. Whenever you are referred to antonyms of a word, it is wise to read the whole entry.

If you turn to the entry HARD and look only at the antonyms, you may be puzzled to find words like limp and tender along with easy and simple. But read the whole entry. What synonym is the opposite of limp? What is the opposite of simple?

23

STRONG WORDS and WEAK WORDS

Sometimes in an entry a word is described as "stronger" or "weaker" than another word. This means that both words express a degree. In other words, they tell how much or how many or how far or to what extent. For example, *hot* is stronger (and warmer) than *warm*. *Roar* is stronger (and louder) than *whisper*. *Cool* is not as strong as *cold*. *Chilly* is weaker than *cold* or *icy*. *Soaking* is stronger (and wetter) than *damp*. *Excellent* is stronger than *good*. *Exhausted* is a stronger word than *tired*. (Although if you were exhausted, you would feel weaker than if you were just tired.) A stronger word shows more feeling about something (even about being tired) or shows a greater degree of something than another word. For example, *guffaw* is a lot stronger than *laugh* because it shows more feeling and a greater degree of loudness.

PRECISE, Exact, or Sharp Words

When the children at the beginning of this book were talking about synonyms, remember how Bill and Jack and Tom *shouted*, *agreed*, and *added* what they wanted to say? These words showed how the boys spoke and helped you see them as they

talked. These are precise words. *Precise* means correct or exactly right. For example, suppose you had a colossal toothache, and the dentist said, "I'll have to pull a tooth." He could start at one side of your mouth and keep pulling teeth until he found the one that ached. But you'd hope he'd be more precise. You'd want him to examine all your teeth and find the exact one that hurt before he began pulling any!

To a careful writer, precise, sharp words are essential tools.

Suppose you saw this sentence written on a piece of paper:

He went into the room and put the book on the table.

This sounds a little like the beginning of a story, doesn't it? But you don't know what kind of a story, or who "he" is, or even whether or not the story is interesting enough to read more. Suppose, however, the sentence read:

He stormed into the room and slammed the book on the table.

or

He staggered into the room and dropped the book on the table.

or

He sneaked into the room and slipped the book on the table.

25

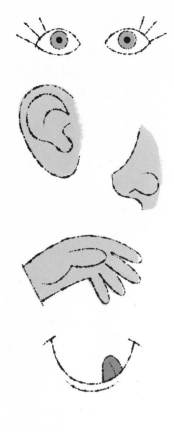

Would you read on? Would you wonder who was angry enough to storm in and slam the book down? Would you wonder why someone was sneaking or staggering? Of course you would! You would want to find out what was really happening.

Slammed, dropped, and *slipped* are not synonyms. They don't all mean the same thing. But they certainly draw sharp, clear pictures, don't they?

A speaker or writer will try to choose words that make the listener or reader almost see, hear, feel, smell, or taste what is being described. Some words can say a lot more than other words.

Look up the entry GO and see a whole page of words that say *go*.

By the way, how many words do you ever use instead of *said*? Can you think of five—fifteen—fifty? You are smart if you can think of fifteen. You are quick-witted if you think to look up the entry SAY (or the word *said*) and count the synonyms. You are well-nigh a genius if you have already looked at the end sheets of this book (the inside parts of the covers) and have noticed that what you see is not just a design!

2

Synonyms
and
Antonyms

ABOUT

ABOUT is a word that is easy to use when you are not sure just when something will happen or when it has happened. You might say you are **about** ready to go home, or that it is **about** time to leave the party. You usually have supper **about** six o'clock. You saw a good TV show **about** a week ago.

Use the word **about** also when you are not sure how much or how many of something. *I drank **about** a quart of milk. She must be **about** a hundred years old. Just **about** everyone went to the game.* You may know a man who seems to be **about** seven feet tall. Some dogs look as if they were **about** three feet long.

about

almost

You can use **about** to tell how far something is. *The airport is **about** five miles away. I walked **about** a mile down the road.*

Almost or ***nearly*** might be used if you mean not quite. *__Almost__ everyone was laughing. I __almost__ won the race. The show was **nearly** over by the time we got to the theater. It was **nearly** dark when he got home.*

Approximately is a good word to use if you don't know whether something is a little more or a little less. *It will cost **approximately** ten dollars to fix my bike.* (It may cost seven dollars or twelve dollars.) *My watch is **approximately** right.* (It may be a minute fast or a minute slow.) You wouldn't say that ***approximately*** everyone was laughing, because there couldn't be more than everyone. You could say that it would cost ***almost*** or ***nearly*** ten dollars to fix the bike. But then you would mean it might cost eight or nine but not more than ten dollars.

well-nigh

Practically, virtually, and ***well-nigh,*** all may be used to mean something so nearly true that the difference doesn't matter. You may be ***practically*** certain of something. A job may be ***virtually*** impossible to do. You may be ***well-nigh*** exhausted after running home.

29

ABSORBING	Look up INTERESTING.
ACHE	Look up HURT.
ADD	Look up SAY.
ADMIRE	Look up LIKE.
AFFECTION	Look up LOVE (n).

AFRAID

AFRAID means feeling fear. The word can be used in many ways. If you are just a little worried about something, not really feeling much fear, you might say you are *afraid* you'll miss the bus or you are *afraid* it's getting late or you're *afraid* you just can't eat another piece of pie. You might feel fear when a certain thing happens or is about to happen. *The girl was afraid when she discovered she was late. We were afraid when we saw a bad storm coming.* Or you might always feel fear of something. *All my life I have been afraid of the dark. Many people are afraid of thunder and lightning.*

Very often *afraid* is used in regular conversation without meaning that you feel fear at all. *I'm afraid you can't come in right now. I'm afraid I don't understand what you mean. I'm afraid you're wrong about that.* This is just a polite way of saying, "You can't come in" or "I don't know what you're talking about" or "You're wrong."

There's one thing to notice about *afraid.* You can say a person or an animal is *afraid,* but you would never say "That is an *afraid* person" or "The *afraid* cat ran away." The synonyms for *afraid* which are listed and described on the next page can be used both ways.

frightened

30

timid
frightened
scared
terrified

Timid means always shy and not willing to do anything daring or bold or dangerous. A *timid* person is not sure he can do or say the right thing. *The boy was too **timid** to jump into the pool. The **timid** girl spoke so softly no one could hear what she said.* A *timid* person is not fearless or confident.

Frightened and *scared* are used when something has caused you to be afraid. *We were more **frightened** by the lightning than by the thunder. He ran like a **scared** rabbit.*

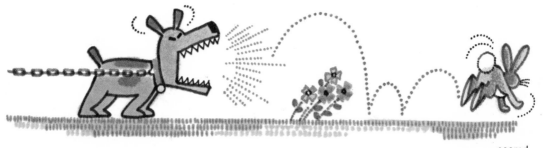

scared

Terrified means shocked and trembling because something has suddenly made you very much afraid. You may be *terrified* by something that might hurt you. *The **terrified** child began to scream when the lights went out suddenly.*

ANTONYMS: bold, fearless, confident, unafraid

AGED   Look up OLD.

AGOG   Look up EXCITED.

AGREE   Look up SAY.
              Look up antonyms of FIGHT.

AID   Look up HELP.

aged

31

AIN'T	AIN'T is a word that causes boys and girls a lot of trouble. The trouble doesn't come from how they use *ain't.* It comes because they use it.
	Even though many, many people say ***ain't,*** there probably isn't a schoolteacher in the country who wouldn't frown at a pupil who used this word in class or who wrote it in a paragraph. Not many years ago— a hundred or so—***ain't*** was perfectly good. Almost everyone said it. Many writers used it a lot. But nowadays you will be better off (and safer!) if you say "isn't" or "aren't" or "am not" or "hasn't" or "haven't" instead.

ALARM	Look up SCARE.
ALMOST	Look up ABOUT.
ALONE	Look up LONELY.
AMBLE	Look up WALK.
AMUSING	Look up FUNNY and INTERESTING.
ANCIENT	Look up OLD.

almost

ancient

32

ANGRY	Look up MAD.
ANNOYED	Look up MAD.

ANSWER (n)

An ***answer*** is anything said or done as a result of something asked or done. You hope you will get an ***answer*** when you call someone on the telephone. When you write a letter to a friend, you look for an ***answer.*** You had better be sure your ***answer*** to a math problem is correct. If you ask a question, you expect an ***answer.***

reply
response
retort
solution

A ***reply,*** like an answer, tells you something you have asked or wondered about. *When we asked to go to the movie, the **reply** was "No." I wrote to some museums asking about dinosaurs, and already I have received three **replies.***

A ***response*** is an answer. Often it is not an answer in words. It is the way you act when something makes you feel glad or sad or angry or eager to do something. *When the man finished his speech, the **response** was a cheer from all of us. Her only **response** to the question was a gasp. There was no **response** when I rapped on the door.*

A ***retort*** is a quick, sharp answer. It may be clever or funny. Sometimes a ***retort*** is sharp and angry. *"May we come in?" we asked the old lady. "No, you may not!" was her loud **retort.***

A ***solution*** is the answer to some problem or puzzle. *The riddle had two **solutions,** but we only found one. The mystery story was so puzzling that I didn't know until the last page what the **solution** was going to be. We have finally found a **solution** for the problem.*

ANTONYMS: question (n), problem

reply

ANSWER (v)

ANSWER means speak or write or do something as a result of what someone asks or wants or needs. When a person speaks to you, you **answer.** You **answer** a letter by writing to the person who sent it to you. If the doorbell rings, you **answer** by opening the door. You **answer** the phone by saying "Hello."

reply
respond
retort
solve

Reply means answer. To **reply to** what someone says, you must think of what you are saying or doing. An echo could not **reply to** someone's shout, but it could answer. You usually **reply** with words. *When he asked me to wait, I **replied** that I would.* You can also **reply** with an action. *When the enemy attacked, the soldiers **replied** with gunfire.*

You **respond** to something either by words or action. If something or someone makes you angry or happy, you may **respond** by stamping a foot or by jumping with joy. If a friend invites you to a party, you may **respond** eagerly, "I'd love to go!" When a clown does a trick in the circus, people **respond** by laughing or clapping. Firemen **respond** quickly when the fire alarm rings.

Retort means answer quickly and sharply. Sometimes a person **retorts** to an unkind or unpleasant remark with another. If someone tells you that your hair needs combing, you may **retort** angrily that hers doesn't look very nice either.

Solve means explain something that has been unknown or find the answer to a problem. *We haven't **solved** the problems of traveling to the moon yet. Do you think you can **solve** the match trick in ten minutes? His sudden appearance **solved** the mystery.*

ANTONYMS: <u>ask</u>, <u>question</u> (v)

respond

34

ANTIQUE   Look up OLD.

antique

APPEAR   Look up COME.

APPROACH   Look up COME.

APPROPRIATE   Look up RIGHT.

APPROXIMATELY   Look up ABOUT.

ARGUE   Look up FIGHT and TALK.

ARID   Look up antonyms of WET.

ARRANGE   Look up PUT.

ARREST   Look up STOP.

ARRIVE   Look up COME.
                        Look up antonyms of GO.

argue

arrive

ASCEND   Look up antonyms of FALL.

ASK   ASK means try to get information. *He **asked** a question. They **asked** what time it was. We **asked** the way to the library. She **asked** her father if he would be home early.* **Ask** or **ask for** also means try to get something from someone. *I **asked** my brother to help me. **Ask** the bus driver **for** change when you get on. We all **asked** our parents if we could go to camp this summer.*

beg
coax
request
inquire
demand

Beg means ask over and over for something you want very much. It may be for something you do not expect to get, or for something you don't really deserve. *The boy **begged** for another chance, but it was denied. The child **begged** for more candy. Every night my dog sits next to the table and **begs** for food. She **begged** her brother not to go out in the storm.*

Coax means ask or try to persuade someone to do what you want. Often you **coax** someone by offering him something or promising to give him something. You **coax** a friend to walk to the store with you. Perhaps your friend will respond by going along— especially if you have money to buy candy.

coax

Request usually means ask for something or ask someone to do something. *He requested an immediate reply to his letter. We were requested to fasten our seat belts.*

Inquire means ask questions to learn about something. *A stranger was inquiring about our neighbor's car. The man came to inquire about the house for sale.*

Demand means ask for something that you mean to get. *The robbers demanded money from the stagecoach passengers. Father demanded an explanation when we were late. I demanded an apology, but she refused to give one.*

ANTONYMS: answer (v), reply (v), refuse, respond

ASSEMBLE   Look up MAKE.

assemble

ASSIST	Look up HELP.
ASTONISHING	Look up WONDERFUL.
ATE	ATE is the past tense of EAT.
ATTEND	Look up COME.
ATTRACT	Look up PULL.
ATTRACTIVE	Look up BEAUTIFUL.

attract

AWFUL

awful

horrible
terrible
dreadful
severe

AWFUL is a word that has suffered from overwork for many, many years. At first, *awful* meant awesome or full of awe. *Awe* means great fear or wonder. An *awful* sight or an awesome sight was one that filled people with fear and awe and wonder. For example, people who lived ages ago and who didn't know anything about nature would look at an eclipse of the sun or moon and think that the end of the world was surely coming. Seeing a volcano erupt is an awesome or *awful* sight, even today. But now people have changed the meaning of *awful* and have used it to describe a lot of things which other words could describe better. They use *awful* when they mean anything hard or unpleasant. It seems easier to use *awful* than try to think of a better word. Rainy weather is *awful.* A bad cold is *awful.* A hard arithmetic problem is *awful.* A spooky movie is *awful.* A dull book is *awful.* His handwriting is *awful.* Sometimes people even say, "Thanks an *awful* lot."

Here are some good words to use if you want to let poor old *awful* have a little rest.

Horrible and *terrible* mean very, very unpleasant and almost painful. *Making a promise I couldn't keep was a **horrible** mistake. In the movie the **horrible** monster grabbed the man. Sam took a **terrible** fall out of the apple tree. Her nightmare was so **terrible** she woke up screaming.*

When something seems dangerous or frightening, it is *dreadful.* *Being caught in a snowstorm overnight was a **dreadful** experience.*

Severe can mean causing great pain and trouble. A cold winter is *severe.* A *severe* toothache is no joke.

38

awful

BAD

BAD is a word that everybody overworks. Anything that is not good may be called **bad.** But a careful writer tries to find other words to tell more sharply what he means.

If your dog is so glad to see you that he jumps on you with dirty feet, you may call him a **bad** dog. You may talk about a **bad** cold, a **bad** storm, a **bad** temper, a **bad** accident. You may call stealing **bad,** or a report card **bad,** or a banana that is too ripe **bad,** or a selfish child **bad.**

naughty
harmful
severe
spoiled
poor
wrong

Naughty describes someone who behaves badly or does something bad that he knows he shouldn't do. A **naughty** child may run and hide when his mother says it's bedtime. Taking a piece of candy after you are told not to would be **naughty.**

Harmful describes something bad that might hurt someone or damage something. Staying out in the sun too long could be **harmful** to your health. Too much smoke in the air is **harmful** to a person's lungs. Washing your clothes with very strong soap can be **harmful** to the cloth.

Severe can describe something that is very bad because it is painful or hard to stand. A *severe* storm may cause damage to gardens, may flood streets and basements. A *severe* cold wave may cause animals and plants to freeze. Someone with a *severe* illness may have to stay in bed a long time.

Spoiled describes several things. *Spoiled* food is bad because it has been kept too long or has become too ripe. A *spoiled* child is one who is used to having his own way about everything.

Poor can mean not as good as something could or should be. A *poor* movie may be badly made or it may be boring. A *poor* throw in basketball probably would miss the basket. Your teacher may think most excuses for not doing your homework are *poor.*

Wrong means bad because it is not right. Giving *wrong* directions to a stranger in town would be as bad as giving none. It's bad to do something you know is *wrong.*

wrong

For other words you might be able to use instead of BAD, look up AWFUL, CARELESS, DANGEROUS, DIRTY, SAD, SCARY. Also look up antonyms of CLEAN, GREAT, KIND, RIGHT.

41

BAMBOOZLE	Look up GYP.
BAR	Look up SHUT.

bar

BATTLE	Look up FIGHT.
BEAUTIFUL	BEAUTIFUL is the opposite of <u>ugly</u>. Anything that is very pleasing or delightful in some way is *beautiful.* You may speak of a *beautiful* baby or a *beautiful* sky or a *beautiful* fairy tale or *beautiful* manners.

pretty
handsome
attractive
lovely

Pretty is not as strong a word as *beautiful.* It describes something that is pleasing to look at but is not large enough or important enough to be called *beautiful.* Something small and delicate or dainty is often called *pretty.*

A brilliant sunset or a bridge, soaring across a river, or a snow-topped mountain or a skyscraper would probably be called *beautiful,* not *pretty.*

beautiful

42

You would call a nice-looking girl *pretty.* The opposite is <u>homely.</u> You might speak of a *pretty* locket or a *pretty* dress or a *pretty* flower. A house may be painted a *pretty* color. A color that isn't *pretty* might be called <u>ugly.</u>

Handsome is used to describe something or someone too large or important to be called *pretty.* It could be an object or person that is well formed and pleasing to look at but is not small or delicate or dainty. *The handsome old mansion looked dignified and stately in spite of the stores built up around it. The handsome horse looked almost like a statue.* A good-looking boy or man is usually called *handsome* rather than *beautiful* or *pretty.*

handsome

A pleasant sight that catches your eye may be called *attractive.* It attracts and pulls your attention. *While we were shopping, we saw an attractive window display. She has an attractive smile.* A bowl of fresh flowers can make a room *attractive.*

Lovely describes something so beautiful it makes you feel good to look at it or even to think about it. *Today is a lovely day for a hike in the woods. We have a lovely view of the lake from the hotel. The garden looks lovely.* Something the opposite of *lovely*—so <u>ugly</u> that it makes you feel shocked or bad to look at it—would be <u>horrid</u> or <u>hideous.</u>

Before you use the word *lovely,* though, look up the entry LOVELY. That entry may suggest some other words you'd rather use.

ANTONYMS: <u>homely, plain, ugly, unattractive, horrid, hideous</u>

BEDLAM	Look up NOISE.
BE FOND OF	Look up LIKE.
	Look up antonyms of HATE.
BEG	Look up ASK.
BEGAN	BEGAN is the past tense of BEGIN.
BEGIN	Look up START and SAY.
	Look up antonyms of END (v) and of STOP.
BEGINNING	Look up antonyms of END (n).

beginning

BEGUN	BEGUN is the past participle of BEGIN.
BEHELD	BEHELD is the past tense and past participle of BEHOLD.
BEHOLD	Look up LOOK.
BELIEVE	Look up THINK.
BIG	When something is called *big,* it may be *big* in size or in importance. A *big* dog can jump over a fence, but a little dog can't. A *big* decision or a *big* problem is one that is very important and must be carefully thought about.

44

gigantic

You can picture a *big* mountain, a *big* crowd, a *big* ice-cream cone. But you know, of course, they are not all the same size. ***Big*** is a word that can be used to describe almost anything that is bigger than something else. But some other excellent words are just begging to be used.

A mountain may be *immense* or *majestic*.
An ocean is *vast*.

A crowd is often *huge, great, enormous,* or *tremendous*. *Huge, gigantic, colossal, large,* all are good words to describe something that is very *big* in size.

A *big* city is large but it is also *important*. Someone who is a *big* help on a project is *valuable* and quite often *necessary* or *essential*.

A *big* parade is usually *grand* or *magnificent; thrilling* or *exciting*.

A *big* athlete is *great, excellent, skilled;* he is *necessary* or *valuable* to his team or school.

A *big* movie star is *famous, well known,* and *important*. Sometimes he is *great*.

Look up LARGE and GREAT and IMPORTANT.

famous

45

BILK	Look up GYP.
BLANK	Look up EMPTY.
BLAST OFF	Look up GO.
BLEAK	Look up COLD.
BLOCK	Look up SHUT.
BOISTEROUS	Look up LOUD. Look up antonyms of QUIET (adj).
BOLD	Look up BRAVE.
BOLT	Look up RUN.
BORING	Look up antonyms of FUNNY and of INTERESTING.
BOUGHT	BOUGHT is the past tense and past participle of BUY.
BOUND	Look up JUMP.

blast off

bound

BOUNDARY	Look up END (n).
BRAVE	BRAVE is the opposite of cowardly. **Brave** means able and ready to face danger. A **brave** man may be afraid, but he still won't run. He is not cowardly.

46

brave

bold
courageous
fearless
gallant
heroic

Bold means not only ready but eager to face danger. A lion tamer in a circus has to be *bold.* No timid man could train wild animals.

A *courageous* person will not only face danger but will do whatever he believes is right or is his duty, no matter what may happen to him. The *courageous* person often is the one who refuses to do something that he believes is wrong. A boy who refuses to go along with his friends when they are doing something he thinks is wrong is *courageous.* A *courageous* person is not afraid to say "No." He is not afraid that his friends will laugh at him.

Fearless people are not shaken by danger. They are not faint-hearted. A fireman is *fearless* when he goes into a burning building to rescue people.

Gallant and *heroic* mean brave and willing to fight against all odds, whether you win or lose—sometimes even when you know you can't win.

Brave and these synonyms describe people, but they can also describe the things people do. Knights did many *brave* deeds. An adventure may be *bold.* A rescue is *courageous.* A speech can be *fearless.* Many *gallant* and *heroic* deeds are done by everyday people.

ANTONYMS: cowardly, faint-hearted, timid

47

BREAK

BREAK means suddenly come apart, or force something to come apart. A dish **breaks** if you drop it. A cook **breaks** an egg to open it. When a water pipe **breaks,** it has to be repaired. *I broke my arm when I fell off the swing. She **has broken** her pencil.*

crack
shatter
smash
crush
fracture
tear
burst
explode
damage
demolish
destroy
wreck

Crack means break but not into pieces. A stone may **crack** the windshield of a car, but the glass will not fall out. A piece of wood can **crack** without falling apart. You can **crack** your mother's best dish.

Shatter is break into many small pieces.

Smash means break by force, too, but not always into pieces. For example, a driver who hit a tree might **shatter** or **smash** his windshield. He might **smash** his fender, but he would not **shatter** it.

Crush means break into tiny pieces by grinding. People **crush** ice. Machines **crush** stones. **Crush** also means squeeze together or push into the ground. *He **crushed** his hat when he sat on it. The dog **crushed** the flowers in our garden.*

Fracture is usually used to mean break a bone. If you fall out of a tree, you may **fracture** your leg.

Tear is break apart by pulling or yanking. Catching a sleeve on a nail will make it **tear.** If you **tear** cloth, you can mend it with needle and thread. If you **tear** a piece of paper, you can mend or fasten it together with tape.

Burst and **explode** are used when something breaks violently and sometimes noisily from some force inside it. A balloon **bursts** if you blow too much air into it. A firecracker **explodes.** *When we were blowing up balloons yesterday, one of mine **burst.***

48

Damage usually means hurt or break an object so that it is not worth as much as if it were perfect. A bad windstorm may *damage* a roof by blowing off shingles so that it will leak. You can *damage* a table or chair by dropping it and breaking off one leg. Something that has been *damaged* can usually be repaired or fixed.

Demolish, destroy, and *wreck* mean tear down or break so completely that an object cannot be fixed. *The men demolished the old building so a new one could be built. The enemy soldiers destroyed everything in sight when they captured the village. He wrecked his car when he hit a tree.*

demolish

Some of the synonyms for *break* are so precise that writers use them to describe other actions which have nothing to do with breaking. For example, you might *burst* into a room to announce good news. Dad *explodes* when you leave your bike in the driveway. Your baseball team might have *smashed* the opponents. Your hopes are sometimes *shattered.* You may find some other words you can use if you look up CUT.

ANTONYMS: fix, repair, mend, fasten

BRIGHT

sunny
shiny
brilliant
flashing
sparkling
glistening
glittering
gleaming
glowing
dazzling
glaring
light
vivid
gay
loud

BRIGHT is the opposite of dim. **Bright** means either sending out light, like the sun, or reflecting it, like the moon.

A **sunny** day is one bright with sunshine. A cloudy day is gray and dark.

An object is **shiny** when it has been cleaned and polished or rubbed until it is bright. It is not dull or dingy.

Brilliant means brighter than usual. *The jewel looked **brilliant** against her dark gown. Stars look **brilliant** on a cold, clear night.*

Flashing and **sparkling** mean sending out quick bursts of light. A **flashing** light comes from just one place, like a turn signal or the light on a police car. A **sparkling** light comes from different spots on a surface—like snow **sparkling** in the sunlight.

Glistening and **glittering** are wonderful words. Say them. You'll hear that **glistening** sounds slippery, and **glittering** sounds hard and cold. A wet street or something covered with oil is **glistening.** Cold, bright stars at night or pieces of broken glass in the sunlight are **glittering.**

glistening

50

Gleaming and *glowing* describe a steady light. A *gleaming* lantern shines through the darkness. A *glowing* fire makes a room warm and cozy.

Dazzling and *glaring* mean bright enough to hurt the eyes. Sunlight on snow is *dazzling*. Car headlights are sometimes *glaring*.

glaring

Light is the opposite of dark. The sky may be *light* blue in the early morning and dark blue at night. A full, bright moon can make the night so *light* you can see to read a book.

Vivid is stronger than light. It means bright because of strong color. Her dress was a *vivid* shade of green, not a faded color.

Gay means bright and merry. *She seemed to have a gay time at the party.* But *gay* may also mean cheerful and bright in color. *The room was painted a gay yellow.*

Loud can mean too bright in color to be attractive. A necktie with *loud* red stripes may look funny.

See SMART (adj) for more words you could use.

Also see the antonyms of DIM and of STUPID.

ANTONYMS: dim, dark, dull, shady, faded, dingy

BRILLIANT	Look up BRIGHT and SMART (adj). Look up antonyms of DIM and of STUPID.
BRING	Look up CARRY.
BRISTLY	Look up ROUGH.
BROAD	Look up antonyms of THIN.
BROKE	BROKE is the past tense of BREAK.
BROKEN	BROKEN is the past participle of BREAK.
BROUGHT	BROUGHT is the past tense and past participle of BRING.
BUDDY	Look up FRIEND.
BUILD	Look up MAKE.
BUILT	BUILT is the past tense and past participle of BUILD.

bristly

build

BULKY	Look up antonyms of LITTLE and of THIN.
BUMPY	Look up ROUGH. Look up antonyms of SMOOTH.

bumpy

BURNING	Look up HOT.
BURST	Look up BREAK. BURST is the same in the past tense and in the past-participle form.
BURY	Look up HIDE.
BUSHY	Look up antonyms of THIN.
BUST	Look up BREAK for better words to use.
BUY	Look up GET.

buy

CALL	Look up SAY and SHOUT.
CALM (v)	Look up antonyms of SCARE.
CALM (adj)	Look up QUIET (adj). Look up antonyms of MAD and of EXCITED.
CAME	CAME is the past tense of COME.
CAPTURE	Look up CATCH.
CAREFUL	Look up antonyms of CARELESS.
CARELESS	CARELESS means not careful. A *careless* child does not think or care about other people's things or even his own things. He may leave his coat or hat or

careless

bicycle on the ground somewhere and then go off and forget it. Losing your lunch money on the way to school is usually *careless*. A *careless* classmate may borrow your eraser, then forget to return it at the end of the day.

reckless
hit-or-miss
sloppy
thoughtless

Reckless means getting into danger without thinking or without having to. A *reckless* bicycle rider does not obey traffic laws. Cautious riders do.

Hit-or-miss means not caring or planning how you do something or how well you have done it. A *hit-or-miss* job is one you hurry to finish. If you are painting a wall in a *hit-or-miss* way, your brush hits parts of the wall and misses parts, but you don't bother to go back and paint the places you missed.

Sloppy can mean careless about how you look or how you do something. *Her clothes were wrinkled, and they looked sloppy.*

This is sloppy Handwriting

Thoughtless means not caring or thinking about what you are doing. It also means not caring about how others feel. Slamming the door when you know someone is sleeping nearby is a *thoughtless* thing to do. You might have said something to a friend which hurt her feelings or made her mad. If you didn't mean to, and only said it without thinking how it would sound to her, you were being *thoughtless*.

ANTONYMS: careful, thoughtful, watchful, cautious

55

CARRY

CARRY means hold something while you move. *The cat **carried** her kitten across the street. Then she dropped it in the grass. The movers **have carried** all the furniture outside. Will they leave it there?*

bring
take
transport
fetch
tote
deliver

You **bring** a package if you carry it from some other place to where you are now.

You **take** a package if you carry it from where you are now to some other place. ***Bring** your camping equipment to my house tonight, and I'll **take** it to school for you tomorrow.*

Transport means move or carry something or someone from one place to another—a bus ***transports*** passengers; a truck ***transports*** objects. *Before railroads were built across the country, pioneers **transported** their furniture to the West by wagon trains.*

Fetch means go and get. A dog ***fetches*** a stick when you throw it. *Jack and Jill were supposed to **fetch** water from the well.*

Tote is used by people in some parts of the country to mean carry in your arms or on your shoulders or on your back. *Students **tote** their books to school. Sailors **tote** their clothes in duffel bags. They carry the bags on their shoulders.*

Deliver means bring or send to a person or place. *When can you **deliver** the groceries we ordered this morning? He had to get up early in the morning to **deliver** his papers.*

Look up SEND. You may find more good words for what you want to say.

ANTONYMS: leave, drop, let go

transport

CARVE

Look up CUT.

56

CATCH

CATCH means get or take hold of something that has been moving or hiding. You might *catch* a ball (if you don't miss), *catch* fish, *catch* a glimpse of someone, or even *catch* a cold. You *catch on* to the way a new game is played. You *catch up* with someone ahead of you. In olden days men *caught* animals for food. Explorers in many lands *have caught* strange animals.

rope
net
trap
snatch
grab
seize
capture

Rope, net, and *trap* mean catch an animal by getting it into something it can't get out of. Out on the range a cowboy *ropes* a calf if he throws a loop around the calf's neck and pulls it tight. Fishermen *net* fish when they throw a big net overboard from a boat and then pull it back full of fish. You would *trap* mice with a mouse trap or *trap* bears with bear traps. *Trap* is often used to mean catch or stop a person or animal. *Police* ***trapped*** *the escaped tiger when it ran into a shed. We* ***were trapped*** *when the elevator stopped between floors. Firemen had to come and free us. The man knew at once that his own statement* ***had trapped*** *him.*

Snatch, grab, and *seize* mean quickly and suddenly take hold of something. *The dog* ***snatched*** *the little girl's candy bar before she knew what was happening. The mountain climber* ***grabbed*** *a rope when he felt himself falling. The man* ***seized*** *the growling dog by the collar.*

Capture means catch or take by force. *The pirates* ***captured*** *the ship and* ***seized*** *the crew and all of the valuable cargo.*

See GET for other words you might want to use.

capture

ANTONYMS: free, let go, miss

57

CAUGHT	CAUGHT is the past tense and past participle of CATCH.
CAUSE	Look up MAKE.
CAUTIOUS	Look up antonyms of CARELESS.
CEASE	Look up STOP.
CHASE	Look up RUN.
CHAT	Look up TALK.
CHEAT	Look up GYP.
CHEERFUL	Look up HAPPY. Look up antonyms of SAD.
CHEERLESS	Look up COLD.
CHILLY	Look up COLD.
CHIP	Look up CUT.

caught

CHOOSE

CHOOSE means decide to take or do one thing instead of another. You *choose* a library book that you want to read. Instead of going to the library on the bus, you may *choose* to walk and refuse to ride. If it rains, you may be sorry you *chose* to walk. You hope you *have chosen* a good book.

select
pick
elect

Select means choose and decide on after you have thought carefully about reasons for taking one thing instead of another. Perhaps in a store you look at the candy on the counter and then *select* the kinds you like best. In a supermarket, shoppers *select* the ripest, reddest apples and throw aside the others. When you buy a pair of shoes, you try several on before you *select* the pair you want and reject the others. *Both dresses were pretty, but the girl **selected** the blue one.*

select

pick out

Pick and *pick out* mean choose from many just what you want. When someone offers you jelly beans, perhaps you *pick* all black ones. When a group chooses sides for a game, each captain tries to *pick* the best players. The first person to get on a bus can *pick out* the best seat. You *pick out* the most exciting book you can find on the shelf.

Pick on is an idiom meaning give trouble to one who can't fight back. A bully *picks on* smaller children.

Elect usually means choose a person for a job by voting for him. More than one person is needed to *elect* someone. Actually more than half of a group must vote for someone in order to *elect* him. *The class **elected** you to speak for us in the meeting.*

ANTONYMS: leave, refuse, throw aside, reject

CHOP	Look up CUT.
CHOSE	CHOSE is the past tense of CHOOSE.
CHOSEN	CHOSEN is the past participle of CHOOSE.
CHUCKLE	Look up LAUGH.
CHUM	Look up FRIEND.
CLAMOR	Look up NOISE.

CLEAN	CLEAN is the opposite of <u>dirty</u>. A **clean** object is one that is new or that has been washed or that has no dirt or spot on it.
neat	*Neat* means clean and also in order or in place. A girl's hair might be clean but mussed up and <u>untidy</u>. It is *neat* if it is clean and combed.
spotless *unspotted* *unstained*	*Spotless, unspotted,* and *unstained,* all mean without any dirt, spots, or stains.
pure *spick-and-span*	*Pure* means without anything added to it or put in it that would cloud, spot, or spoil the object or make it <u>impure</u>. Water is *pure* if it is not <u>polluted</u> by germs. *Pure* air in a city becomes <u>polluted</u> when chimneys pour out smoke. A lump of *pure* gold has no clay or sand mixed with it.
	You have a *spick-and-span* room if it has just been cleaned and tidied up.
	ANTONYMS: <u>unclean</u>, <u>dirty</u>, <u>soiled</u>, <u>untidy</u>, <u>filthy</u>, <u>polluted</u>, <u>grimy</u>, <u>impure</u>

CLEAR	Look up antonyms of DIM.
CLEVER	Look up SMART (adj). Look up antonyms of STUPID.
CLIP	Look up CUT.
CLOSE	Look up END (v) and SHUT. Look up antonyms of START.
CLUMP	Look up WALK.
COARSE	Look up ROUGH. Look up antonyms of SOFT.
COAX	Look up ASK.

clip

COLD

COLD is the opposite of hot. Something *cold* has a temperature lower than things nearby. If you picked up two bottles of pop and one of them felt *cold,* you would know it had just been taken from the refrigerator. *Cold* may also be an antonym of kind or friendly. Some people seem *cold* and *unfriendly* when you first meet them.

cool
chilly
frosty
icy
unfriendly
bleak
cheerless

Cool and *chilly* mean not quite cold. *Cool* means pleasantly and comfortably cold. *The cool breeze felt good after the sun went down. The weather was cool and rainy. Chilly* is unpleasantly cold but not so cold you can't stand it. *The room became chilly when the fire died down. It was too chilly to go swimming.* The difference between these two words is that it is pleasant to feel *cool.* It is not pleasant to feel *chilly.* Warm is their antonym.

Something is *frosty* if it is covered or looks as if it is covered with frost. Grass may be *frosty* on a cold autumn morning. When windows are *frosty,* you can't see through them.

Something *icy* is covered with ice or filled with ice or feels like ice. A street may be *icy.* A river gets *icy* in winter. An *icy* wind makes you cold.

Cold and its synonyms are often used to describe something or someone *unfriendly. The lady gave me a frosty glance when I stepped in front of her. We were so late we received a cool welcome from our friends. His smile was chilly.*

Bleak and *cheerless* mean cold and unfriendly and unpleasant. An old house, high on a cold, windswept hill, looks *bleak.* A bare room is *cheerless.*

ANTONYMS: hot, warm, torrid, sweltering

icy

61

COLLAPSE   Look up FALL.

collapse

COLOSSAL   Look up LARGE.

COME   COME means move from some other place to
where you are. It is the opposite of go. Your
teacher may say, *"Come to school early tomorrow."*
Perhaps you *came* home late yesterday. Or you
had just *come* into the room when the bell rang.
Some of these other words aren't really synonyms
for *come,* but often they may be used in place of it
when you want to show a special meaning.

arrive   *Arrive* means come to a certain place. *I hope you
enter   will **arrive** at my house before the others have to
attend   leave. The train **arrived** at one o'clock and departed
approach   at half-past two. After a long winter we were glad
appear   to see spring **arrive.**
loom
            Enter can mean come into a place. You *enter* a
building. In a play an actor *enters* when he comes
onto the stage. *We saw her immediately when
she **entered** the room. But she left before we had
a chance to speak to her.*

Attend can mean come to or be present at something.
*The Pilgrims **attended** church in Plymouth.*

62

Twelve people will **attend** *our meeting. Only seven* **attended** *the last one.*

Approach means come near or toward something. *Soon we will* **approach** *a bend in the road.* An airplane descends gradually and **approaches** the runway before it lands.

Appear means come into sight. A person can **appear** at a window or around a corner. A boat **appears** over the horizon. Spots may **appear** on your face if you get the measles. They will disappear when you are well again. **Appear** can also mean "seem to be." *The girl* **appeared** *timid as she stood up to speak. There* **appears** *to be no mistake in his work.*

appear

Loom means come into sight or appear. But it usually is used when something appears in dim or foggy light and looks larger than it really is. *Suddenly, as we stumbled in the darkness, the tree* **loomed** *in front of us. The sailors were frightened when another ship* **loomed** *out of the fog right in front of them.*

ANTONYMS: go, depart, leave, disappear

COMICAL	Look up FUNNY.	
COMMENT	Look up SAY and TALK.	
COMMON	Look up antonyms of QUEER.	
COMMOTION	Look up NOISE.	
COMPANION	Look up FRIEND.	
COMPEL	Look up MAKE.	
COMPLETE	Look up END (v).	
COMPLICATED	Look up HARD.	
COMRADE	Look up FRIEND.	

comical

CONCEAL	Look up HIDE.
	Look up antonyms of SHOW.
CONCLUDE	Look up END (v) and STOP.
	Look up antonyms of START.
CONCLUSION	Look up END (n).
CONFIDENT	Look up antonyms of AFRAID.
CONSERVE	Look up KEEP.
CONSIDER	Look up THINK.
CONSIDERATE	Look up KIND.
CONSTRUCT	Look up MAKE.
CONSUME	Look up EAT.
CONTENTED	Look up HAPPY.
	Look up antonyms of SAD.
CONTINUE	Look up SAY.
	Look up antonyms of STOP.

conceal

construct

COOL	LOOK up COLD. Look up antonyms of HOT and of EXCITED.
COÖPERATE	Look up HELP.
CORRECT	Look up RIGHT.
COURAGEOUS	Look up BRAVE.
COVER	Look up HIDE.
COWARDLY	Look up antonyms of BRAVE.
CRACK	Look up BREAK.
CRAMMED	Look up FULL. Look up antonyms of EMPTY.
CRANKY	Look up MAD.
CRAZY	Look up MAD and STUPID.
CREAMY	Look up SMOOTH.
CREATE	Look up MAKE and START.
CROSS	Look up MAD.
CROWDED	Look up FULL. Look up antonyms of EMPTY.
CRUEL	Look up antonyms of KIND.
CRUISE (v)	Look up GO.
CRUISE (n)	Look up TRIP.
CRUSH	Look up BREAK.

coöperate

crush

CUT

CUT means open, divide, or take away with a sharp-edged or pointed tool. You **cut** a watermelon to open it. *My mother has baked two pies today and* **has cut** *one of them in pieces. Yesterday you* **cut** *a flower from its stem.*

These words describe some other ways to cut.

clip
snip
carve
slice
slit
slash
peel
saw
chop
chip

Clip and **snip** mean cut with short strokes of scissors or some other sharp edge. Usually you **clip** or **snip** small objects like hair or thin material like cloth. A barber **clips** short hairs off a boy's neck. A dressmaker **snips** the edge off a piece of cloth. She **snips** off a thread. A gardener **snips** off rosebuds, and he **clips** a bush.

Carve can mean cut carefully to form something. An artist **carves** a figure from a piece of wood. You might **carve** a rose out of a cake of soap. You would not **carve** a rose off a rosebush.

Carve and **slice** also mean cut by moving a knife back and forth through something. You **carve** meat when you cut it into pieces for serving. You **slice** bread or meat when you cut thin, flat pieces from a loaf or a roast. You have **slit** a board if you have cut it lengthwise or in long, thin pieces. *The tailor* **slit** *cloth when he made a long cut in it.*

To open a letter you **slit** the envelope along the fold at the top.

Slash means make heavy, deep cuts without being careful where the cuts fall. Explorers **slash** through a jungle when they swing heavy, sharp knives against the vines and underbrush. If an artist became angry with his work, he might destroy a painting by **slashing** it with a knife.

carve

chop

You *peel* potatoes when you cut away the skins.

You *saw* a piece of wood by cutting it with back-and-forth strokes of a sharp saw.

Chop means cut in pieces with many short, hard blows—a man *chops* wood with an ax. Cooks *chop* vegetables.

You *chip* a piece of ice or a rock if you cut off small pieces from the edges. *He **chipped** the stone until it fit into the hole.*

You may find other words for what you want to say if you look up BREAK.

CUTE

CUTE is a tired word. People use it too often. They could say what they really mean if they stopped to think of accurate words. Before using *cute,* look up some of these other words and see if you don't find one that fits better!

A *cute* puppy is *naughty, friendly, comical.*

A *cute* baby may be *beautiful, attractive, bright,* or *happy.*

A *cute* trick may be *clever* or *unusual* or *funny.*

A *cute* movie might be *amusing, interesting, entertaining, hilarious,* or just *pleasant.*

A *cute* boy or girl is probably *attractive, agreeable, thoughtful, friendly,* and not ugly or unpleasant, cross or irritable.

A *cute* dress may be *attractive, pretty, bright, dainty.*

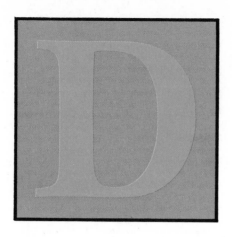

DAINTY	Look up antonyms of ROUGH.
DAMAGE	Look up HURT and BREAK.
DAMP	Look up WET.

DANGEROUS

DANGEROUS means apt to cause injury or harm or loss unless great care is taken—an illness can be *dangerous.* Riding a bicycle on a dark street may be *dangerous.* An escaped lion is *dangerous.*

unsafe
risky
hazardous
precarious

Unsafe means not free from danger or from the risk of injury. Thin ice is *unsafe* for skating. A leaky boat is *unsafe.* A bicycle with bad brakes is *unsafe.*

Risky, hazardous, and *precarious,* all mean something is uncertain because there is a chance of danger, and you may not be safe or succeed in what you do. It is *risky* to visit someone who has measles—if you might catch them. Ice on the streets makes driving *hazardous.* You could find yourself in a *precarious* position if you climbed a tall tree or ladder and then couldn't get down.

ANTONYMS: safe, harmless

68

DARK	Look up DIM. Look up antonyms of BRIGHT.
DART	Look up FLY.
DASH	Look up HURRY.
DAWDLE	Look up antonyms of HURRY.
DAZZLING	Look up BRIGHT. Look up antonyms of DIM.
DECEIVE	Look up GYP.
DECLARE	Look up SAY.
DELIBERATE	Look up antonyms of FAST (adj).
DELIBERATELY	Look up antonyms of FAST (adv).
DELICATE	Look up antonyms of ROUGH.
DELIGHTED	Look up HAPPY. Look up antonyms of SAD.
DELIGHTFUL	Look up WONDERFUL.
DELIVER	Look up CARRY.
DEMAND	Look up ASK.
DEMOLISH	Look up BREAK. Look up antonyms of MAKE.
DEMONSTRATE	Look up SHOW.
DEPART	Look up GO. Look up antonyms of COME.
DEPOSIT	Look up PUT.
DESCEND	Look up FALL.
DESERTED	Look up EMPTY.

descend

DESOLATE	Look up LONELY.
DESPISE	Look up HATE.
DESTROY	Look up BREAK. Look up antonyms of MAKE.
DETEST	Look up HATE.
DEVOTION	Look up LOVE (n).
DEVOUR	Look up EAT.
DIFFICULT	Look up HARD.
DIG UP	Look up FIND.

dig up

DIM

DIM can be the opposite of bright. An object or a thought or a sound that is not clear may be called **dim.** The light inside a cave is **dim.** You might have only a **dim** idea of how to make a pie. *His voice sounded **dim** and far away.*

dull
shady
shadowy
dark
misty
smoky
foggy
gloomy
faded
muffled
faint

Dull means not clear or not shining and bright. You might think that gray is a **dull** color and yellow is a gay color. Bright red is vivid. On a **dull** day the sky is cloudy. If the sun suddenly comes out, it may be dazzling. Thunder booming in the distance makes a **dull** sound.

Shady, shadowy, and **dark** mean that some of the light has been cut down or cut off in some way. *The willow tree gave us a **shady** place to eat our picnic lunch. As we sat around the campfire after supper, Rob noticed two **shadowy** figures come out of the forest and walk toward us. When the moon went behind a cloud, the night was **dark.** We could hardly see a thing in the **dark** cave.*

70

Misty and *smoky* are often used to describe air that is not clear. The air gets *smoky* when people burn leaves. Near a waterfall the air is *misty*. *We carried flashlights through the misty night so we could find our campsite.*

Foggy describes air so full of mist you can hardly see through it. *We went through the foggy streets without even seeing the people ahead of us.* You might also use *foggy* to mean that your thoughts are mixed up or not clear. *He was still a little foggy about following the directions we gave him.*

Gloomy means dim and dark and cheerless. *The room looked gloomy when all the windows were shut and the curtains were drawn.*

When something has become less bright and less colorful than it was, it is *faded.* *The scarecrow in the field wore an old faded suit and a tattered hat.*

Muffled and *faint* describe sound that has been softened or deadened in some way. *The muffled voices behind the closed door sounded angry. The faint sound of music came through the night. Faint* also describes a sight or thought that is not plain. *The faint outline of a mountain in the distance told the sailors they were nearing the shore. I had only a faint idea of what the word meant.*

See the antonyms of BRIGHT for other words you might be able to use.

ANTONYMS: bright, brilliant, radiant, clear, glowing, shiny, gleaming, dazzling, vivid, gay

faded

DIM-WITTED   Look up STUPID.
Look up antonyms of SMART (adj).

DIN	Look up NOISE.
DINGY	Look up DIRTY.
	Look up antonyms of BRIGHT.
DIRECT	Look up SHOW.

direct

DIRTY

soiled
spotted
stained
filthy
grimy
smeared
smudged
dingy
impure
polluted

DIRTY is the opposite of clean or pure. Your clothes usually get *dirty* when you play outdoors.

Soiled means dirty because of being worn or used for some time without being washed. A shirt or a dress that has been worn for several days becomes *soiled.* Clothes in a store that have been tried on by many people often become *soiled* before anyone buys them.

Spotted and *stained* mean unclean because something has been put on or spilled on. Your dress or shirt may be *spotted* if you are careless about eating an ice-cream cone and let it drip. *Leaky pens cause many stained fingers.*

Filthy and *grimy* are stronger words meaning dirty. A house that is not cleaned very often becomes *filthy. The children's clothes were filthy after they had played in the mud. His socks were so grimy his mother had to wash them twice. We peeked through the grimy window of the deserted barn.*

Smeared and *smudged* often mean dirty because of careless handling. A picture is *smeared* if someone has touched the paint before it was dry. If you spill a drop of paint or ink on a picture and then try to rub it off, you may *smear* the whole thing. If your hands are very dirty when you write, your paper will probably be *smudged.*

Dingy means dirty and without brightness or color. *The old woman lived in a **dingy** room. The house looked **dingy** until we painted it.* If you start to mix some water colors and get too much black or brown in, you may end up with a *dingy* gray.

Impure and *polluted* mean not clean or pure because of dirt being put into something. It is dangerous to drink water that may be *impure.* Rivers and lakes are often *polluted* by dead fish or by garbage.

ANTONYMS: clean, pure, spick-and-span

DISAGREE   Look up FIGHT.

disagree

DISAGREEABLE   Look up MAD.

DISAPPEAR	Look up GO. Look up antonyms of COME.

disappear

DISCARD	Look up antonyms of KEEP.
DISCLOSE	Look up antonyms of HIDE.
DISCONTINUE	Look up STOP.
DISCOVER	Look up FIND. Look up antonyms of HIDE.
DISCUSS	Look up TALK.
DISGRUNTLED	Look up MAD.
DISGUISE	Look up HIDE.
DISGUSTED	Look up MAD.
DISLIKE	Look up HATE. Look up antonyms of LIKE.
DISPATCH	Look up SEND.
DISPLAY	Look up SHOW.
DISPUTE	Look up FIGHT and TALK.

discover

74

DIVE	Look up JUMP.
DIVED	DIVED is the past tense and past participle of DIVE. DOVE is also the past tense of DIVE.
DOVE	DOVE or DIVED is the past tense of DIVE.
DOWNCAST	Look up SAD. Look up antonyms of HAPPY.
DRAG	Look up PULL.
DRAW	Look up PULL.
DRAWN	DRAWN is the past participle of DRAW.
DREADFUL	Look up AWFUL.
DRENCHED	Look up WET.
DREW	DREW is the past tense of DRAW.
DRIVE	Look up PUSH.
DRIVEN	DRIVEN is the past participle of DRIVE.
DROP	Look up FALL and END (v). Look up antonyms of CARRY.
DROVE	DROVE is the past tense of DRIVE.
DRY	Look up antonyms of WET.
DUG	DUG is the past tense and past participle of DIG.
DULL	Look up DIM and STUPID. Look up antonyms of BRIGHT, of SMART (adj), of INTERESTING, and of FUNNY.
DUMB	Look up QUIET (adj) and STUPID. Look up antonyms of SMART (adj).

dive

EAGER   Look up EXCITED.

EARN   Look up GET.

EASY   Look up antonyms of HARD.

EAT   EAT means take in through the mouth, chew, and swallow. *We **ate** breakfast early.* ***Have** you ever **eaten** bear meat?* ***Eat*** can also mean destroy by wearing away or taking away a little at a time. A strong acid will ***eat*** through something it has been spilled on. A river can ***eat*** or wear away its banks and form a canyon.

consume ***Consume*** means eat a large amount. *The crowd at a*
devour   *ball game can **consume** hundreds of hot dogs.* ***Consume***
feed   can also mean destroy. *The fire **consumed** the log.*
graze   ***Devour*** means eat greedily. A hungry lion in the zoo
nibble   ***devours*** his meat. If you were so hungry you ***devoured***
gnaw   five doughnuts, you would have stuffed them into
gobble   your mouth and eaten them as fast as you could.
gulp   If you were so hungry you ***consumed*** five doughnuts, you would have eaten them all, but we wouldn't know how fast or how hungrily you ate them.

76

feed

Many different words may be used to describe how animals eat. We use some of these same words to tell how people eat.

Horses *feed* on hay or grain. Many large fish *feed* on smaller fish.

Cows and horses in a pasture *graze* when they bite off and eat grass. *In summer flocks of sheep graze on the mountainside.*

A rabbit *nibbles* on a lettuce leaf when it eats small bits at a time. *The girl sat and nibbled at her apple.*

A dog *gnaws* a bone when he wears it away by biting on it for a long time. Have you ever eaten meat that was so tough you had to *gnaw* on one piece for ten minutes?

Gobble means eat fast and greedily.

Gulp means drink in large swallows or swallow food without stopping to chew. *He gulped two pieces of candy before his mother saw him.*

Whenever you were hungry enough to eat five doughnuts—whether you *devoured* them or *consumed* them—you probably *gobbled* the first one, but when you came to the last one, you *nibbled* it.

gobble

nibble

EATEN	EATEN is the past participle of EAT.
ELDERLY	Look up OLD.
ELECT	Look up CHOOSE.

elect

EMPTY	EMPTY is the opposite of <u>full</u>. **Empty** means having nothing inside. Something may be *empty* because what is usually in it or what you would expect to find inside is not there. An *empty* house is one with no furniture or people in it. An *empty* desk has nothing in it. An *empty* gas tank has no gas in it. You may have an *empty* feeling by evening if you forgot or didn't have time to eat some lunch.
vacant *deserted* *blank* *hollow*	**Vacant** means empty but especially means having no person in it. A *vacant* house is unoccupied, with no one living in it, though it may have furniture. Motels rent *vacant* rooms to travelers at night. A *vacant* seat is one with nobody sitting in it.

vacant

78

If you have ever sat staring into space with your thoughts far away, you might have been accused of having a *vacant* stare.

Deserted can mean left empty and uncared for. A *deserted* house is empty when the people who lived there have moved away and no one else wants to move in. *Deserted* houses very often look as though they might be haunted.

Blank usually describes a surface that has no mark on it. A *blank* space in a test or an exercise is a space to be filled with the correct answer. A *blank* page in a book is one with no writing on it. A *blank* wall has no doors or windows in it and no pictures hanging on it. A person who starts to say something and suddenly forgets what it was might explain that his mind suddenly "went *blank*."

Hollow means having a hole inside. A *hollow* tree is one in which the inside has rotted away, leaving the trunk empty. A garden hose is a *hollow* tube. A soda straw is *hollow*.

ANTONYMS: full, crammed, crowded, occupied, packed

deserted

ENCOURAGE   Look up PUSH and HELP.

END (n)

limit
boundary
tip
conclusion
finale
outcome
result
goal
purpose

END means the very last point to which something can go. It is the opposite of the beginning or outset.

Limit means a point that you can not or may not go beyond—a speed *limit,* a time *limit* in a game.

A *boundary* usually is a line that marks the end or limits of a piece of land. The *boundary* of a country is where its land ends and another country's land begins. A fence often marks the *boundaries* of a yard or a farm.

Tip means a pointed end of something small—the *tip* of your nose or *tip* of a finger or *tip* of a pencil.

Conclusion means the end of something that has been done or has happened. *We won't know the conclusion of the story until next week.*

Finale is usually used for the end of a musical piece or the last part of a stage performance. *Everyone in the show took part in the finale. The finale was loud, with trumpets blowing and drums thundering.*

Outcome and *result* are what happens at the end of something you do or hope for or work for. Both could be good or bad. The *outcome* of a story might be that the prince and princess lived happily ever after. *Winning a prize in a music contest is usually the result of much practice.*

Goal is an end or result that you work for. *Her goal in life was to be a singer.* When you reach the *goal* in a game, you have won or are safe.

Purpose is like *goal* but usually means a reason for doing something. *His purpose in writing the note was to ask for help.*

finale

ANTONYMS: beginning, outset

80

END (v)

END means the opposite of start. It means stop doing something, or come to the point where there is no more. The game **ended** in a tie. The rain started at dawn but **ended** before noon.

finish
conclude
complete
close
stop
drop

Finish, conclude, complete, mean bring to the end whatever you have started to do. A poet **finishes** a poem when he has written all of it. A doctor **concludes** his examination when he has done everything necessary to find out what is wrong with a sick person. A workman **has completed** a job when he has done all the things he was hired or paid to do. You can use **conclude** to mean come to an end. You might say, "The book **concludes** with a beautiful wedding scene." But you wouldn't say a book **finishes** or **completes** with a wedding scene.

Close means end something by limiting the time. *The contest **closed** at midnight. We found the popcorn stand **had been closed** for the winter. It will open again in the spring.*

Stop means end suddenly what you are doing, whether it is finished or not. You **stop** a game you have just started when you are called to supper. You **stop** writing when you **have finished** a story. *The audience **stopped** talking when the curtain went up.*

Drop can mean end something suddenly and maybe forever. You end an argument when you **drop** the subject and introduce a new one. *The project that was launched last year **was dropped** when the State Government ran out of money. The boys were willing to **drop** everything and go fishing.*

Look up STOP for other words you might use.

ANTONYMS: begin, open, start, launch, introduce

close

81

ENEMY	Look up antonyms of FRIEND.
ENJOY	Look up LIKE. Look up antonyms of HATE.
ENJOYABLE	Look up WONDERFUL.
ENORMOUS	Look up LARGE.
ENRAGED	Look up MAD.
ENTER	Look up COME.
ENTERTAINING	Look up FUNNY and INTERESTING.
ENTHUSIASTIC	Look up EXCITED.
ESCAPE	Look up GO.
ESSENTIAL	Look up IMPORTANT.
ESTABLISH	Look up MAKE and START.
EVEN	Look up SMOOTH.
EXAMINE	Look up LOOK.
EXASPERATED	Look up MAD.
EXCELLENT	Look up GOOD.

examine

EXCITED   EXCITED can be the opposite of quiet. *Excited* means feeling strongly about something and showing your feeling. You may be indifferent to something that you don't feel *excited* about. Your feeling may be good or bad. You are *excited* about having a vacation. In an argument you might get *excited* when you should keep cool. You'd be pretty *excited* if a fire engine stopped in front of your house. Anyone would be *excited* to hear he won a prize or to hear that a tornado was coming. He might look calm, though.

eager
agog
impatient
enthusiastic

Eager means wanting to do a certain thing or being very much interested in something. *He is **eager** to go to the party. As she passed the dish of candy, she saw the child's **eager** face.*

Agog means filled with excitement about something that is going to happen. *We were all **agog** when we heard he was coming.*

Impatient means excited and unwilling to wait for something. *Waiting for the rain to stop made us **impatient**.*

Enthusiastic means eager and excited about something. *The class was **enthusiastic** about our new project and couldn't wait to begin.*

ANTONYMS: calm (adj), cool, indifferent

EXCITING   Look up INTERESTING.

EXCLAIM   Look up SAY.

EXCURSION   Look up TRIP.

EXHIBIT   Look up SHOW.

EXPEDITION   Look up TRIP.

expedition

EXPLODE   Look up BREAK.

FABULOUS	Look up WONDERFUL.
FADE	Look up GO.
FADED	Look up DIM. Look up antonyms of BRIGHT.
FAINT	Look up DIM.
FAINT-HEARTED	Look up antonyms of BRAVE.
FAIR	Look up RIGHT.

FALL

FALL means move downward or become less or lower. *Leaves **fall**. The man's voice rose, then **fell**. After the flood the river **had fallen.***

tumble
topple
drop
descend
sink
collapse

Tumble means fall suddenly, maybe rolling over and over. *A boy climbing a tree may lose his hold and **tumble** to the ground.*

Topple means fall because of too much weight on top. *If you stack books too high, they will **topple**. The chimney was so tall that people were afraid it would **topple** when a strong wind blew.*

Drop means fall swiftly or unexpectedly or let something fall. *When he turned his bank over and*

84

*shook it, some money **dropped** out. She was carrying so many papers she **dropped** them.* You also can **drop** your voice to a whisper or **drop** your eyes by looking down or **drop** off to sleep.

Descend can mean move or go downward. Airplanes **descend** before they land. When they take off, they ascend. Deep-sea divers **descend** to the bottom of a lake. *The path **descends** sharply to the water's edge. The king **descended** the stairs slowly.*

Sink means fall or become lower, sometimes slowly. A stone **sinks** when it falls to the bottom of a lake. The sun **sinks** as it sets.

sink

Collapse means fall apart or fall into pieces. Something you are building or putting together may **collapse** if it is not done right. If a person falls down because he is too tired or sick to stand, he **collapses**. *After a hundred years the old barn **collapsed**.*

ANTONYMS: rise, ascend

FALLEN	FALLEN is the past participle of FALL.
FALSE	Look up antonyms of RIGHT.
FAMOUS	Look up IMPORTANT.
FASCINATING	Look up INTERESTING.
FASHION	Look up MAKE.

FAST (adj)

FAST is the opposite of slow. As an adjective, *fast* means able to move from one place or position to another in a very short time. A *fast* runner can get home safely. A baseball player can make a *fast* catch or a *fast* throw.

fast

rapid
swift
speedy
quick
hasty
sudden
instant

Rapid means fast in movement. A *rapid* river flows fast. A sluggish river moves slowly.

Swift means fast or happening suddenly. *He took a swift look around the room. There was a swift change of plans.*

Speedy means able to move rapidly or to get something done very fast. *The speedy boy was back before we knew it.* A poky boy makes everyone wait for him. You would speak of a river as *rapid* or *swift*. You would not call it *speedy*.

Quick means fast in learning or understanding or doing something. *He gave a quick answer to the question. He was quick about understanding and doing his work.* If you are in a hurry, you may have a *quick* lunch. If you are not in a hurry, you probably have an unhurried dinner.

Hasty means in a hurry and perhaps too fast to be carefully thought out. A *hasty* decision may not be as good as a more deliberate one.

86

sudden

Sudden and **instant** mean happening or acting very fast. They are the opposite of gradual. You can make **instant** pudding in a very short time. A bus may have to come to a **sudden** stop, but usually it slows down and comes to a gradual stop.

Fast can also mean held tight. *The door is stuck **fast**.*

ANTONYMS: slow, sluggish, poky, gradual, deliberate, unhurried

FAST (adv)

As an adverb, **fast** tells how something or someone moves. *One boy ran **fast**. The others walked slowly. My watch was running **fast**, not slow.* Its synonyms have the same meanings as the synonyms for the adjective **fast**.

rapidly
swiftly
speedily
quickly
hastily
suddenly
instantly

*The river runs **rapidly** or **swiftly**, not sluggishly.*

*Get your work done **speedily** so we can go.*

*She decided **quickly** or **hastily**, not deliberately.*

***Suddenly** we were scared. It had gradually been getting darker. I dropped the hot pan **instantly**.*

Fast can mean tightly when it tells how you do something. *Hold **fast** to the rope. Tie the boat **fast** to the dock so it won't float away.*

If you are not quite sure why **fast** is used both as an adjective and an adverb, this may help. The adjective tells what kind of person or thing you are describing. The adverb tells how someone or something does something. For example, a boy may be a **fast** or a **swift** runner. But you'd say he ran **fast** or **swiftly**.

ANTONYMS: slow, slowly, sluggishly, gradually, deliberately

FASTEN	Look up antonyms of BREAK.
FAT	Look up antonyms of THIN.
FEARLESS	Look up BRAVE. Look up antonyms of AFRAID.
FED	FED is the past tense and past participle of FEED.
FEEBLE	Look up antonyms of STRONG.
FEED	Look up EAT.
FELL	FELL is the past tense of FALL.
FETCH	Look up CARRY and GET.
FEUD	Look up FIGHT.
FIERY	Look up HOT.

fiery

FIGHT   FIGHT means struggle against someone or something. People may *fight* by hitting each other, or they may *fight* with words. Sometimes boys *fight* on the playground. Medicine *fights* infection. *The plane **fought** head winds all the way.* Many soldiers **have fought** in two wars.

disagree	When people **disagree,** they have different ideas or points of view. *The girls agreed to have a party but* **disagreed** *on what day to have it.*
argue	
dispute	
squabble	**Argue** means offer reasons for your point of view. Two people who disagree on something may **argue** all day and still not change each other's mind. You can disagree with someone without arguing.
quarrel	
quibble	
feud	**Dispute** means argue angrily or question what someone thinks. *I told the child that eight o'clock was his bedtime, but he* **disputed** *me. The ranchers* **disputed** *the farmer's right to build a fence.*
oppose	
battle	
war	

Argue means offer reasons for your point of view. Two people who disagree on something may **argue** all day and still not change each other's mind. You can disagree with someone without arguing.

Dispute means argue angrily or question what someone thinks. *I told the child that eight o'clock was his bedtime, but he* **disputed** *me. The ranchers* **disputed** *the farmer's right to build a fence.*

Squabble and **quarrel** mean argue noisily. *The children* **squabbled** *over who should go first. It is foolish to* **quarrel** *with your neighbors.*

Quibble means argue about something that is not very important. *The two girls* **were quibbling** *over whether the glass was half full or half empty.*

Feud means quarrel with another family or group for a long time. *The two families* **feuded** *over the boundaries of their farms for many years.*

Oppose means be against or object to something. It is stronger than disagree. *I* **oppose** *your plan to charge admission to the children's zoo.*

Battle and **war** mean fight or struggle violently. *The teams* **battled** *for first place. You* **battled** *a cold all winter. The armies* **warred** *against their enemies. Indians* **warred** *against the settlers.*

ANTONYM: agree

battle

FILTHY   Look up DIRTY.
           Look up antonyms of CLEAN.

FINALE   Look up END (n).

FIND

FIND means come upon something you may have lost and are looking for or come to know something you didn't know before. *Did you ever **find** the book you misplaced? She **found** that the word was too hard. **Have** you ever **found** a lost dog? I tried to hide my sister's birthday present where she wouldn't **find** it.*

discover
unearth
uncover
dig up
locate

Discover means find something that has been there but no one has known about before. An explorer **discovers** new lands. *I discovered a hole in my shoe.*

Unearth, uncover, dig up, mean bring to light something that may be unknown or lost or forgotten. A farmer's plow might **unearth** an Indian arrowhead. A policeman may **uncover** a secret plot to rob the bank. You may **dig up** an old hat from the attic to wear to a costume party.

Locate means find the position or place of something. You **locate** the North Pole on a map. *He finally **located** a gas station. If I lose my friend's address, I'll never be able to **locate** him.*

ANTONYMS: lose, misplace, hide

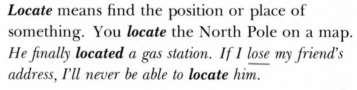
locate

FINE	Look up LITTLE and THIN. Look up antonyms of LARGE and of ROUGH.
FINISH	Look up END (v.). Look up antonyms of START.
FIRM	Look up HARD. Look up antonyms of SOFT.
FIT TO BE TIED	Look up MAD.
FIX	Look up antonyms of BREAK.
FLASHING	Look up BRIGHT.

finish

90

FLAT	Look up SMOOTH.
FLED	FLED is the past tense and past participle of FLEE.
FLEE	Look up RUN.
FLEECY	Look up SOFT.
FLEW	FLEW is the past tense of FLY.
FLIGHT	Look up TRIP.
FLIMSY	Look up antonyms of STRONG.
FLING	Look up THROW.

fling

FLIT	Look up FLY.
FLOAT	Look up FLY.
FLOWN	FLOWN is the past participle of FLY.
FLUFFY	Look up SOFT.
FLUNG	FLUNG is the past tense and past participle of FLING.
FLURRY	Look up NOISE.
FLUSHED	Look up HOT.
FLUTTER	Look up FLY.

flutter

FLY

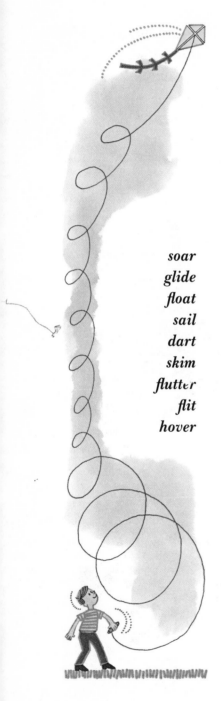

FLY means move through the air with the help of wings. Birds and airplanes *fly*. *Birds **flew** south last fall. They **have flown** over our house every year.* *Fly* also means make something move through the air. Pilots *fly* airplanes. Children *fly* kites. Many people *fly* the flag on July 4. But we also use *fly* to mean move fast and easily. *She **flew** to answer the doorbell. The days **fly** by. The boat seemed to **fly** over the water.*

We use many other words to mean move swiftly or easily, even though they are not synonyms of *fly*.

soar
glide
float
sail
dart
skim
flutter
flit
hover

Soar, glide, float, and *sail* all mean move easily. A bird *soars* when it flies upward in the sky. A baseball *soars* when it is hit up over the fence. A bird can *glide* through the air without moving its wings. An ice skater seems to *glide* over the ice. *Float* and *sail* mean move on the surface, but we say clouds *float* across the sky or the ball *sailed* over the fence. *She seemed to **float** down the stairs.*

Dart and *skim* mean move quickly from place to place or just above a surface. A hummingbird *darts* from flower to flower. A rabbit may *dart* from a hollow log and disappear down a hole. A low-flying plane *skims* over the trees. A sailboat *skims* over the water.

Flutter and *flit* mean move quickly from one place to another, sometimes with nervous, jerky motions. Leaves *flutter* to the ground, just as a bird *flutters* around in a cage. A scrap of paper seems to *flutter* along the street on a windy day. *A wounded duck **fluttered** along the ground. A hungry* bird **flits** *from branch to branch. Some children* **flit** *from one toy to another.*

Hover means hang in the air almost without moving. A bird **hovers** in the air until he sees a fish in the water below, then he dives to catch it. Helicopters can **hover** over the ground.

Fly also means escape or run away. *By the time the sheriff's posse arrived, the bank robbers* **had flown** *into the hills.*

See GO and HURRY for other words to use.

FOE	Look up antonyms of FRIEND.
FOGGY	Look up DIM.
FONDNESS	Look up LOVE (n).
FOND OF	Look up LIKE.
FOOLISH	Look up STUPID.
FORCE	Look up MAKE.
FORCEFUL	Look up STRONG.
FORLORN	Look up LONELY and SAD.
FORM	Look up MAKE.
FOUGHT	FOUGHT is the past tense and past participle of FIGHT.
FOUND	FOUND is the past tense and past participle of FIND.
FRACTURE	Look up BREAK.
FRAIL	Look up antonyms of STRONG.
FREE	Look up antonyms of CATCH.

force

FRIEND	FRIEND is someone you like and who likes you. There are many other words people can use instead of *friend* to show more exactly how good a *friend* someone is.

neighbor
comrade
companion
chum
pal
buddy

A *neighbor* really means one who lives near you, but many people think of a *neighbor* as one who is friendly, willing to help you any time you need it, and who expects that you will do the same for him.

A *comrade* is a close friend. But the word did not always mean that. An ancient Latin word "camera" meant a room where someone could stay overnight. In olden days travelers who stopped at an inn often had to share their rooms with several other people. A person who shared your room became known as a "camarada." Just as a "camarada" traveled in different countries, this word traveled into different languages, until finally the meaning and spelling have changed, and *comrade* means a close friend. *Soldiers who fight together are **comrades**.*

A *companion* may be a close friend or one who goes with you. *The two were **companions** on a trip.*

Chum, pal, and **buddy** are other good words for a close friend.

ANTONYMS: enemy, foe

FRIENDLY	Look up KIND.
FRIENDSHIP	Look up LOVE (n).
FRIGHTEN	Look up SCARE.
FRIGHTENED	Look up AFRAID.
FRIGHTENING	Look up SCARY.
FROSTY	Look up COLD.

frightening

94

FULL

FULL is the opposite of empty. It means having or holding as much as possible. A *full* glass of milk has no room for any more to be poured in. A *full* day has every minute taken up with something to be done. A *full* bus has no vacant seats and no place for another rider to stand.

heaping
overflowing
loaded
stuffed
crowded
jammed
crammed

Heaping and *overflowing* mean more than full. A cup so full of sugar that the sugar is piled higher than the cup's edge would be called a *heaping* cupful. When a recipe calls for a *heaping* teaspoonful of cocoa, it means you must use more than just a teaspoon filled to the top with cocoa. If the cup is filled with water or other liquid that cannot pile up but spills over the sides, it is an *overflowing* cup. An *overflowing* river is so full that water is pouring over the banks.

Loaded means filled or covered with something. A *loaded* ship is one that has been filled with whatever cargo it is to carry, and has no room for anything more. A *loaded* gun has bullets in it. *Our apple tree was **loaded** with blossoms this spring.*

Stuffed means filled by being packed tightly. After a big dinner you may feel *stuffed.* Many pillows are *stuffed* with feathers. *Stuffed* animals are cloth toys made for small children. The opposite of *stuffed* is hollow.

Crowded, jammed, and *crammed* mean uncomfortably full. A *crowded* room may have too many people in it, or it may be filled with too much furniture. When a bus has so many people on it that they can hardly move, it is *jammed. That closet is so **crammed**, we can't get another thing in it.*

ANTONYMS: empty, hollow, unloaded, vacant

loaded

FUNNY

amusing
entertaining
humorous
witty
laughable
comical
hilarious
ludicrous
ridiculous

FUNNY describes something different from everyday things or something unexpected enough to cause laughter and entertainment.

An *amusing* story catches your attention in a pleasant way, makes you listen, and usually makes you laugh.

An *entertaining* story holds your attention, too. It is not boring or dull. But it does not always make you laugh. It may be sad and may make you cry.

Humorous describes anything or anyone that makes you laugh. A *humorous* story or happening may delight you because it is funny. A *humorous* person is one who sees the funny side of things and enjoys it and points it out to others in a kindly way.

A *witty* person is one who is quick to see something funny or strange and to surprise you with it. He may not always be funny. He may even be unkind. A *witty* remark may make you laugh, but it may hurt someone's feelings.

Anything *laughable* makes you laugh whether it is meant to be funny or not. The story he told to explain his mistake was *laughable.* The idea of our team beating the champions was *laughable.*

Comical means funny enough to make you laugh a great deal. *The clown riding backwards on the horse was* **comical.** *Your friend told us a* **comical** *story about your trip.*

Something *hilarious* makes you roar with laughter. It is more than just funny. *We had a* **hilarious** *time at the party.*

A *ludicrous* sight or a *ridiculous* happening makes you laugh, but you often feel pity or scorn rather than pleasure from it. *Such a fat lady trying to squeeze*

96

*into that small space was a **ludicrous** sight. He looked so **ridiculous** with pie all over his face that we had to laugh.*

Look up QUEER for other words you might decide to use instead.

ANTONYMS: boring, dull, sad

funny

FURIOUS   Look up MAD.

GALLANT	Look up BRAVE.
GALLOP	Look up RUN.
GAVE	GAVE is the past tense of GIVE.
GAY	Look up HAPPY and BRIGHT. Look up antonyms of DIM.
GAZE	Look up LOOK.
GENTLE	Look up SOFT and KIND. Look up antonyms of HARD and ROUGH.
GET	GET is the opposite of give. **Get** means come to own or to have something. You can **get** a letter or **get** a present or **get** a dish off the table. It can also mean become. You can **get** older or **get** cold or **get** sick or **get** hit. *We **got** what we wanted for Christmas.* By the way, the words **got** and **gotten** are used—for example, *It **had gotten** quite cold during the night,* or *I **have got** two dimes.* But there are other ways of saying what you mean that will always sound better. You might say *It had become quite cold during the night,* or *I have two dimes.*

receive
obtain
fetch
earn
win
buy
catch

Receive means get something that is <u>given</u> or <u>sent</u> or handed to you. You **receive** mail or information. You could even **receive** a black eye.

To **obtain** something you must try in some way to get it. You may **obtain** a bicycle by buying it or **obtain** a book you want from the library.

Fetch means go and get something and bring or take it somewhere. *Please **fetch** me a glass of water.*

Earn means do some kind of work for what you get or expect to get. *She **earned** money for a trip next summer. She did baby-sitting to **earn** it.*

Win means get something when there is a contest or chance of not getting it. You **win** first prize if you have the lucky number. If you don't have it, you <u>lose</u>. You **won** a race if you beat someone who was racing against you. A champion boxer **wins** his title but has to <u>give</u> it <u>up</u> or <u>relinquish</u> it when he gets beaten.

win

Buy is get something by paying for it. *She will **buy** a hat tomorrow to match the dress she **bought** today.*

Catch is often used to mean get a disease. *I hope you won't **catch** my cold. I **caught** it when I got my feet wet yesterday.*

ANTONYMS: <u>give</u>, <u>send</u>, <u>lose</u>, <u>relinquish</u>, <u>give up</u>

GIANT	Look up LARGE.
GIGANTIC	Look up LARGE.
GIGGLE	Look up LAUGH.
GIVE	Look up antonyms of GET.
GIVEN	GIVEN is the past participle of GIVE.
GIVE UP	Look up antonyms of GET.
GLAD	Look up HAPPY. Look up antonyms of SAD.
GLANCE	Look up LOOK.
GLARE	Look up LOOK.
GLARING	Look up BRIGHT.
GLEAMING	Look up BRIGHT. Look up antonyms of DIM.
GLIDE	Look up FLY.
GLISTENING	Look up BRIGHT.
GLITTERING	Look up BRIGHT.
GLOOMY	Look up DIM.
GLOWING	Look up BRIGHT. Look up antonyms of DIM.
GNAW	Look up EAT.
GO	GO is the opposite of <u>stop</u> and of <u>come</u>. It means start to move or move away from. When you *go* outside or *go* away or *go* swimming, you move from where you are or from doing what you are doing.

give

glowing

100

Spring _comes_ and **goes.** Traffic _stops_ and **goes.**
*You **go** when the traffic light is green. He **went** as
soon as he could. They **had gone** before we arrived.*

leave

Leave usually means go away from some place or
from someone or without something. *A train **leaves**
the station every hour. The boy **left** his friends and went
on alone. She **left** the baby at home.*

depart

Depart also means go away. *This train **departs** at
noon, and another arrives two hours later. The boys
departed without saying good-by.*

progress

Progress can mean go forward. *We **progressed** very
slowly because the traffic was so heavy.*

proceed

Proceed means go along a certain way or by a
certain plan. *We **proceeded** slowly because the tracks
were covered with snow. He **proceeded** to the corner
as he was told to do.*

run

Run sometimes means go or work, when you speak
of a motor or engine. *My watch stopped yesterday,
but it is **running** now. We can't make the record
player **run.***

retreat

Retreat means go back. *The enemy began to **retreat**
when our army attacked.*

escape

Escape means go away or get away from
something. *Gas was **escaping** from the pipe. The
robbers **escaped** from jail.*

Many words that are not really synonyms for **go** can
be used to make your language sharper and
more precise. Turn the page to find a lot of other
good words you might want to use instead.

TURN PAGE

disappear	*Disappear* and *vanish* mean go out of sight,
vanish	or just cease to be. <u>Stay</u> and <u>remain</u> are
fade	antonyms of these words. For example, a plane
melt	*disappears* when it goes out of sight in the sky.
take off	*The fog **disappeared** when the sun came up.* It ceased
blast off	to be. *Vanish* often is used when something
fly	*disappears* suddenly. *I saw a face <u>appear</u>*
stray	*at the window, but it **vanished** instantly.*
cruise	Darkness *vanishes* when you turn on a light.
ramble	*Fade* and *melt* mean disappear or go out of
travel	sight or out of hearing slowly. Colors *fade*

when they become dimmer and dimmer. A sound
can *fade* in the distance. *The TV picture **faded***
*until it was gone. The sound of the whistle **faded** as*
the train sped away. Snow *melts* and *disappears*
in spring.

Take off, blast off, and *fly* mean go off the ground.
Take off and *fly* are sometimes used to mean go fast
and suddenly. *The next plane **takes off** in an hour. The*
*dog **took off** after the rabbit. Two astronauts **blasted off***
yesterday. I can only <u>stay</u> and talk for a minute. Then
*I must **fly.***

Stray means go slowly and wander around
without any particular goal. *The cows **strayed***
across the road and into a field of corn.

Cruise, ramble, and *travel* are good words for *go.*
*The police car **cruised** down the street looking for the*
*lost dog. We **cruised** down the river in our boat. We*
***rambled** all over Grandfather's farm. The cars*
***traveled** slowly through the fog.*

ANTONYMS: <u>arrive</u>, <u>stop</u>, <u>stay</u>,
<u>remain</u>, <u>come</u>

take off

melt

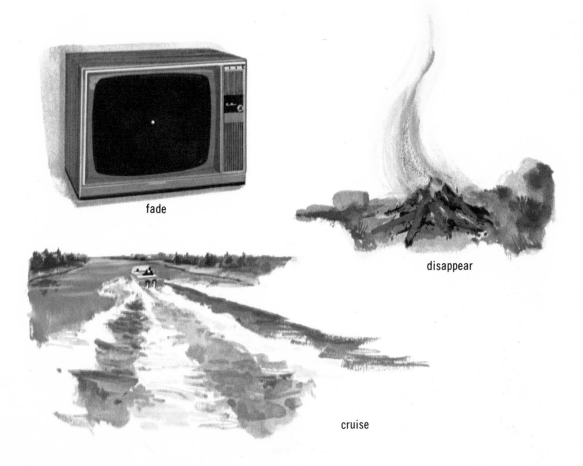

fade

disappear

cruise

103

GOAL	Look up END (n).
GOBBLE	Look up EAT.
GONE	GONE is the past participle of GO.
GOOD	GOOD is the opposite of bad. It is also a word that is used too often and used to describe too many things. Almost anything that pleases you when you see, hear, taste, smell, or touch it may be called *good.* *Good* can describe anything that is useful, right, or pleasant. A pencil with a *good* point is useful. A *good* pupil tries to do his homework right. A *good* day is pleasant. A careful writer or speaker tries to use other words that describe something so clearly that people will know at once what he means.

useful
valuable
pleasant
excellent
skilled
right

pleasant

Useful means ready to be used. A hammer is a *useful* tool for a carpenter. A watch makes a *useful* gift. *My brother gave me some **useful** ideas for earning money.*

Valuable means good enough to be used or taken care of or worth a lot of money. *Valuable* papers must be kept in a safe place. Friends are *valuable* because you wouldn't want to lose them. You would hate to throw away anything *valuable.* Losing a dollar bill makes you unhappy, but it could teach you a *valuable* lesson about taking care of your money.

Pleasant describes something that gives you a good feeling. You enjoy saying "Hello" to someone who has a *pleasant* smile. It is *pleasant* to listen to music that you like. Going to an amusement park can be a *pleasant* way to spend the day. A cool breeze or a glass of cold milk or a swim can all be *pleasant* on a hot day.

excellent

Excellent means more than good when you describe something useful or someone able to do something very well. You may have some *excellent* ideas for a party. A lifeguard must be an *excellent* swimmer. You probably would not speak of having an *excellent* friend or going for an *excellent* walk.

Skilled means able to do something extremely well through much practice. A *skilled* carpenter has built many houses and knows how. A *skilled* mechanic has repaired many cars. A boy who is an *excellent* athlete would probably not be a *skilled* baseball player if he had never played the game.

Right can mean good, to describe things that are not wrong or bad. The *right* answer to a question is a good one. *The **right** thing for the girl to do was admit her mistake. The **right** place to cross a street is at the corner.*

right

For other words you may want to use instead, look up BEAUTIFUL, BRAVE, CLEAN, FUNNY, GREAT, HAPPY, INTERESTING, KIND, RIGHT, SMART (adj), WONDERFUL. Also look up antonyms of CARELESS, DANGEROUS, DIM, DIRTY, MAD, SAD, SCARY, STUPID.

105

GOSSIP	Look up TALK.
GOT	GOT is the past tense and past participle of GET.
GOTTEN	GOTTEN is a past-participle form of GET, but try not to use it very often.
GRAB	Look up CATCH.

grab

GRADUAL	Look up antonyms of FAST (adj).
GRADUALLY	Look up antonyms of FAST (adv).
GRAND	Look up GREAT.
GRAZE	Look up EAT.
GREAT	GREAT means large. Then it is the opposite of little or small. *Great* also can mean important or excellent. Then it is the opposite of petty and trivial. A *great* man may not be big in size, but he may have a brilliant mind. He may have done some outstanding deed or may have served his country well. George Washington was a *great* general. Albert Einstein was a *great* scientist. *Great* baseball players are listed in the Baseball Hall of Fame.

grand
magnificent
majestic
stately
mighty
tremendous
noble

Grand and **magnificent** mean not only large but handsome and dignified and inspiring. *The young king and all his knights in their shining armor made a **grand** sight. He did a **magnificent** job of running the city when he was mayor.*

Majestic and **stately** mean not only great in size but great in appearance and dignity. *The large tree stood **majestic** against the sky. A **stately** procession went slowly down the street.*

stately

Mighty means large and strong or powerful. *A **mighty** river thunders down the mountainside. A **mighty** roar came from the crowd.*

Tremendous means so large and powerful that it causes alarm or wonder or terror. *A **tremendous** earthquake shook the buildings. The **tremendous** elephant pulled a tree out of the ground.*

Noble is great in appearance and action. *A **noble** man is the opposite of a mean or small-minded, selfish man. The man had a **noble** face. Saving a life is a **noble** deed.*

Look up LARGE and IMPORTANT for other words you might use.

ANTONYMS: little, small, petty, trivial, mean

107

GRIMY	Look up DIRTY.
	Look up antonyms of CLEAN.
GRIN	Look up LAUGH.
GROUCHY	Look up MAD.
GUARD	Look up KEEP.
GUESS	Look up THINK.
GUFFAW	Look up LAUGH.
GUIDE	Look up SHOW.
GULP	Look up EAT.

guard

GYP

GYP is an informal word often used to mean keep or take something from someone dishonestly. A clerk in a store may *gyp* you if she doesn't give you enough change (though she might be making an honest mistake). You may feel that you **have been gypped** if you trade an arrowhead for a knife and then find that the knife blade is broken. *A big boy **gypped** me out of first place in line by sneaking in ahead of me. The umpire **gypped** us out of the last run by calling our man out at the plate.*

gyp

cheat
mislead
trick
deceive
bamboozle
swindle
bilk

Cheat means gyp, usually by doing something no one else notices. *He **cheated** at checkers by moving his king when I wasn't looking.*

Mislead means send in the wrong direction or away from the truth. If a street sign has been turned around by some playful boys, it may **mislead** you.

Trick means cheat someone by misleading or fooling him. *The girls **tricked** us into helping them clean up after the picnic by promising us the rest of the chocolate cake. They knew all the time that there was no cake left.*

Deceive and **bamboozle** mean give a false impression in order to fool someone. *The magician **deceived** us by making us think his hat was empty. I was completely **bamboozled** by the boy's friendly smile. Then he hit me.*

bamboozle

Swindle means take money by deceiving someone. *I was **swindled**. I paid fifty cents for this kite and it's not even worth a dime.*

Bilk means not pay someone what you owe. All newspaper boys know what **bilk** means. When you discover that one of your customers has moved away without paying this month's bill, you've been **bilked**.

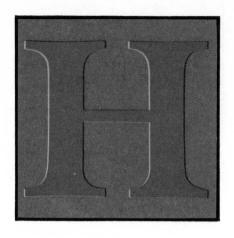

HALT	Look up STOP.
HANDSOME	Look up BEAUTIFUL.
HAPPY	HAPPY is the opposite of sad. *Happy* means feeling well and being contented and pleased with everybody and everything. You may be *happy* when you play with a friend or go to a party or think of a camping trip. Or something can be called *happy* if it makes you feel good. You can have a *happy* vacation or hear the *happy* song of a bird or have a *happy* look on your face.

There are many other excellent words you can use to mean *happy*.

happy

cheerful
lighthearted
glad
delighted
jubilant
gay
jolly
joyful
merry
contented
satisfied

Cheerful means full of good feeling and expecting the best. A person has a *cheerful* disposition if he is usually happy with what he is doing. He is not <u>unhappy</u> or <u>melancholy</u> or always expecting the very worst to happen.

Lighthearted is happy with nothing to worry about. Hearing that you passed a swimming test can make you feel **lighthearted.**

Glad usually means happy because of something good that has happened or will happen. *She was **glad** she went to the party. He will be **glad** to get your letter. I was **glad** to hear the news.*

Delighted is stronger than glad. *Grandmother was **delighted** with her present. The **delighted** girl blew out her birthday candles.*

Jubilant means showing great delight. It is the strongest word for happy. *Everyone in school was **jubilant** when we won the championship.*

Gay, jolly, joyful, merry, mean feeling very, very happy and excited, perhaps laughing and joking. These feelings may not last very long—a person who is not always happy may be *gay* or *jolly* or *merry* at a party. A party can be *gay, jolly,* or *merry,* too.

Contented and *satisfied* mean happy with where you are or what you are doing, not wishing you could go somewhere else or change anything. *She was **contented** in her new house. Our teacher was **satisfied** with the results of our work. This store has many **satisfied** customers.*

ANTONYMS: <u>unhappy</u>, <u>sad</u>, <u>downcast</u>, <u>melancholy</u>, <u>mournful</u>, <u>sorrowful</u>, <u>miserable</u>, <u>wretched</u>, <u>woebegone</u>

jubilant

HARD

HARD is the opposite of easy. It is also the opposite of soft. You might say *hard* means several quite different things.

Hard is the opposite of easy when you speak of something that takes a lot of work or effort. It is *hard* to get out of bed on a cold morning. Cleaning your room is a *hard* job. Scrubbing the floor is *hard* work. Swimming a mile is *hard.* Some people think math is *hard.* Some directions are *hard* to follow.

Hard is the opposite of soft when you say a coconut has a *hard* shell. A wooden bench is *hard.* You probably use *hard* to describe candy you can't bite or a sidewalk you can skate on or paste that has dried in the jar and won't spread.

Hard is the opposite of gentle when you say that there was a *hard* wind blowing or that the villain in the story was a *hard* man.

difficult
complicated
firm
solid
stiff
rigid
tough
severe
stern
harsh

Difficult and *complicated* mean not easy. You might use *difficult* when you talk of a problem or task that makes you use your brain or come to some decision. What to buy with some birthday money may be a *difficult* decision. Writing words on paper is usually not hard, but a good book report can be *difficult* to write. Some books are *difficult* to read, even for a good reader.

Something is *complicated* if it has so many parts that it is difficult to understand or hard to take apart and put together. The works of a clock are *complicated.* A *complicated* explanation gives so many reasons and is so long that you may be more confused after you hear it than you were before. Some *complicated* puzzles are fun to work.

rigid

Firm and **solid** mean hard as the opposite of soft. They mean not easily moved out of place or out of shape. Ice on a pond is **firm** when it is so hard that it does not break or sink when you walk on it. It is **solid** if it is frozen from top to bottom. A **solid** board has no holes or cracks in it.

Stiff and **rigid** mean unbending. They are the opposite of soft and limp. **Stiff** bristles in a brush are not easily bent. Your legs may feel **stiff** after you have sat in one position for a long time. It is hard to walk because they don't move easily. Something **rigid** is so **stiff** it can't be bent without being broken. A steel beam in a building is **rigid**. A board is **rigid**.

Tough means firm and strong but not rigid and unbending. A piece of **tough** meat can be chewed, but it is firm and hard to break apart. Tender meat is easy to chew. We often call a difficult problem **tough**. A **tough** athlete has great endurance.

Severe, stern, and **harsh** mean hard as the opposite of soft or gentle or light. You may consider a person **severe** or **stern** who demands that a thing be done exactly right and does not allow any excuses or reasons for doing it another way. A **severe** punishment can hurt more than a light one. When your father looks **severe** or **stern,** you probably don't argue with him. **Severe** and **harsh** can describe something not gentle or mild. A **severe** winter or a **harsh** wind is unpleasant and causes discomfort to many people.

tough

ANTONYMS: easy, simple, light, soft, gentle, mild, limp (adj), tender

113

HARDY	Look up STRONG.
HARM	Look up HURT.
HARMFUL	Look up BAD.
HARMLESS	Look up antonyms of DANGEROUS.
HARSH	Look up ROUGH and HARD. Look up antonyms of SMOOTH and of SOFT.
HASTEN	Look up HURRY.

hasten

HASTILY	Look up FAST (adv).
HASTY	Look up FAST (adj).
HATE	

hate

HATE may be the opposite of like. **Hate** really means dislike something so much you want to break it or hurt it as much as you can. **Hate** is a very strong word. Actually it is the opposite of love. People often use **hate** when they don't really mean it. You may say you **hate** carrots or **hate** to go to bed early, when you really mean you don't like carrots or you don't like to go to bed early. You may say you **hate** your best friend, but you mean you're a bit angry at him or her right at this moment.

114

dislike	***Dislike*** means not enjoy or not approve of something or someone. *I **dislike** Western movies, but I enjoy stories about cowboys. Cats **dislike** getting wet.*
despise	
detest	
loathe	***Despise*** is stronger than dislike. You usually ***despise*** something if you dislike it and think it is not worth noticing. You ***despise*** a coward.

If you dislike something very much, you **detest** it. You may **detest** doing the dishes but enjoy running the vacuum cleaner. You probably like school but sometimes **detest** homework.

If you shudder at the thought of touching or getting near something, you **loathe** it. Many people—especially girls—**loathe** crawly things. *She **loathed** the task of putting a worm on a fishhook.*

ANTONYMS: love (v), enjoy, like, be fond of

HAUL   Look up PULL.

haul

HAZARDOUS	Look up DANGEROUS.
HEAPING	Look up FULL.
HEAVY	Look up antonyms of THIN.
HELD	HELD is the past tense and the past participle of HOLD.

115

HELP

HELP means supply whatever someone needs or do whatever must be done for him. You **help** a friend with homework or **help** an old person walk. Some medicine **helps** when you are sick. A new belt or collar may **help** the appearance of an old dress. A person in great danger cries **"Help!"** when he cannot do anything to **help** himself.

aid
coöperate
support
assist
improve
encourage

Aid means help, but it is not quite so strong a word. To **aid** someone is to help by adding your work to his in order to do something. Pupils can **aid** in a drive to collect clothes or money. Money will **aid** medical research. Lack of money can obstruct or hinder it. *The Red Cross does everything it can to* **aid** *people who are caught in a flood.*

Two people or nations **coöperate** when they work together on a project or a job that will help them both. States **coöperate** in building highways. *One man not only refused to* **coöperate** *with the committee but promised to oppose everything it did.*

You **support** someone if you help him walk by letting his weight rest on you. *She* **supported** *the sick woman until they found a chair.* **Support** also means help by supplying all the money one needs. A father usually

support

116

assist

supports his family. You **support** someone who is running for office by helping persuade people to vote for him.

Assist means help someone do something by working with him. You **assist** an old person across the street or up the stairs. A librarian **assists** you in finding the books you want. A nurse **assists** a doctor or a dentist by taking care of his instruments.

Improve means help by making something better. *Painting the house* **improved** *its appearance. Salt* **improves** *the taste of some vegetables. Winning this game will* **improve** *our standing in the league.*

Encourage is help by giving hope to someone. *You* **encouraged** *me when you said I played well enough to get in the band.*

ANTONYMS: hinder, obstruct, oppose

HELPFUL	Look up KIND.
HEROIC	Look up BRAVE.

heroic

HID	HID is the past tense of HIDE.
HIDDEN	HIDDEN is the past participle of HIDE.

HIDE

HIDE means put or be out of sight. You can *hide* a pencil or *hide* your face behind your hands. You *hid* yourself when you played hide-and-seek. A thing *may be hidden* on purpose or by accident. In a snapshot one person's head may *hide* another person's face. Birthday presents *can be hidden* until the day of a surprise party.

conceal
disguise
cover
bury
mask

Conceal usually means hide or cover up something on purpose so it won't be discovered. Birds that build their nests on the ground *conceal* them in the grass. *His friend may* *conceal* *the truth to keep him from being caught. His enemy may reveal it.* A general *conceals* his plans from the enemy. A spy can disclose them.

Disguise means change the look of something or someone so it won't be recognized. A young actor *disguises* himself to play the part of an old man. Some people *disguise* their true feelings by acting just the opposite.

Cover can mean hide by putting something over and around. *He* *covered* *his footprints with leaves. Snow* *covered* *the path. He* *covered* *cracks in the wall with paint.*

Bury means hide by covering with a large amount of something. *Pirates* *buried* *treasure in the ground. During a snowstorm people* *might be buried* *in a snowdrift. The newspaper you want* *has been buried* *under a whole pile of papers.*

Mask means hide by making something hard to recognize or see. *The poet* *masked* *his real meaning by using words that mean something else.*

ANTONYMS: disclose, discover, unmask, reveal

conceal

118

HIDEOUS	Look up antonyms of BEAUTIFUL.
HIKE	Look up WALK.
HILARIOUS	Look up FUNNY.
HINDER	Look up antonyms of HELP.

hinder

HIT-OR-MISS	Look up CARELESS.
HOBBLE	Look up WALK.
HOLD	Look up KEEP.
HOLLOW	Look up EMPTY. Look up antonyms of FULL.
HOMELY	Look up antonyms of BEAUTIFUL.
HOP	Look up JUMP.
HORRIBLE	Look up AWFUL.
HORRID	Look up antonyms of BEAUTIFUL.
HORRIFYING	Look up SCARY.

hop

HOT

HOT describes something that feels warmer than things around it or that gives you a burning feeling when you touch, taste, or get near it. *Hot* also means angry. *Hot* is used in many ways—a *hot* day, a *hot* drink, a *hot* temper, a *hot* chase. There are many other words that can be used instead of *hot* even though they are not all synonyms.

fiery
flushed
burning
steaming
warm
tepid
sultry
torrid
sweltering
sizzling
peppery

Fiery means full of fire or flaming. Steel in a blast furnace is *fiery*. *The traveler in the desert could not stand the fiery sun any longer.* Icy winds are sometimes as unbearable as a *fiery* sun. You may say someone who becomes angry very easily has a *fiery* temper. A swallow of food that is loaded with pepper would be *fiery* in your throat. A dragon that blew flames from its mouth could be said to have *fiery* breath.

Flushed means hot and red. Someone's face may be *flushed* if he has a fever or is angry or has just done a lot of running and exercising.

Burning describes something hot enough to be uncomfortable—the *burning* sand on the desert, a *burning* pain in the head.

Steaming is hot enough to turn water into mist. A tub of *steaming* water or a cup of *steaming* cocoa would be very hot. A *steaming* jungle would feel hot and wet and sticky.

Warm means just hot enough to be comfortable or to give comfort. A *warm* coat feels good. A spring wind is *warm*. Cool is the opposite of *warm*.

Something neither hot nor cold may be called *tepid*. Water in a small lake may be *tepid*. Hot food may cool until it is *tepid* and not very pleasant to eat.

steaming

120

Air is *sultry* when it is hot and damp and sticky before a thunderstorm.

Torrid means unbearably hot and dry. *The sun is usually torrid over the desert.*

Sweltering means terribly hot. On a *sweltering* day you feel as though you might burn up. You may be *sweltering* unless you can go swimming.

Sizzling means hot enough to burn or cook with a hissing sound. A frying pan full of *sizzling* bacon sounds and smells good in the morning.

Peppery food is stinging to the taste because it is seasoned with lots of pepper and spices. Many people prefer food that is mild.

ANTONYMS: cold, cool, icy, mild

torrid

HOVER	Look up FLY.
HOWL	Look up LAUGH and SAY.
HUBBUB	Look up NOISE.
HUGE	Look up LARGE. Look up antonyms of LITTLE.
HUMOROUS	Look up FUNNY.
HURDLE	Look up JUMP.

hurdle

HURL	Look up THROW.
HURRY	HURRY means move quickly or make someone or something move quickly. *Hurry so you won't be late. Don't <u>dawdle</u> while you are dressing. We have to* **hurry** *Mother along or we'll surely miss the plane. Can you* **hurry** *your work a little?*

hasten
rush
speed
hustle
dash
fly

Hasten and **rush** mean move or push forward in a great hurry. *The children* **hastened** *to tell their teacher what had happened. Yesterday Father had to* **rush** *through breakfast in order to catch his train. If he <u>had lingered</u> over his coffee one minute longer, he would have missed it.*

rush

Speed sometimes means go very fast. When cars **speed,** they often <u>are slowed down</u> by policemen. *The firemen* **sped** *to the blaze, but traffic delayed them.*

Hustle means force onward quickly. *After breakfast Mother* **hustled** *the children off to school. She told them not to <u>loiter</u> on the way.*

Dash also means move swiftly, but for only a short distance. *He had to* **dash** *to catch the ball before it hit the ground.*

Fly is a good word for hurry. *We'll never make it if we don't* **fly** *the minute school is over.*

ANTONYMS: <u>loiter</u>, <u>slow down</u>, <u>linger</u>, <u>dawdle</u>

122

HURT

HURT has several meanings. It can mean cause pain to the body or to someone's feelings. *I hurt my ankle when I turned it. She hurt my feelings when she said she didn't like my new sweater.*

Hurt can also mean damage something. *Losing the game has hurt our chances of winning the championship this year. I hope the rain won't hurt your new dress.*

Hurt also means feel pain. *My wrist hurts when I try to pick anything up.*

harm
damage
injure
mar
spoil
ache
sting
smart

Harm means give or cause pain. *Telling a lie could harm other people. Nothing can harm you here.*

Damage means hurt or lower the value of something. *Reading for a long time in a dim light can damage your eyes. The heavy truck damaged the small car by hitting it.*

Injure means wound or hurt someone. You might *injure* yourself and others if you're not careful when you ride your bike.

Mar means hurt by changing or spoiling the appearance of something. Smudges will *mar* a newly washed and polished windowpane. *A deep scratch marred the table top.*

Spoil means hurt beyond repair. *I spoiled my soap carving by cutting too deep. Too much pepper spoiled the soup I was making for supper.*

Ache means suffer or feel pain. *The tumble I took down the stairs made my head ache.*

Sting and *smart* mean suffer sharp, quick pain. If you catch a hard ball with your bare hand, your hand will *sting.* Medicine put on a cut finger sometimes makes it *smart* or *sting.*

ache

HUSTLE

Look up HURRY.

ICY	Look up COLD. Look up antonyms of HOT.
IMAGINE	Look up THINK.
IMMENSE	Look up LARGE.
IMPATIENT	Look up EXCITED.

impatient

IMPORTANT	IMPORTANT means very useful or having great worth or value. It is the opposite of trivial. ***Important*** also means great or large. A city or river may

be *important*. A meeting of two kings could be *important* to their people. *The President makes important decisions as well as minor ones every day.* A steering wheel is an *important* part of an automobile.

famous
essential
necessary
valuable

Famous means well known and usually well liked or respected. People often become *famous* for something important they have done or for some important job they hold. All *famous* men are not great or important, but many of them are. *"Liberty and justice for all" are famous words.*

Essential and *necessary* are the strongest words to describe a part so important to something that the thing could not be or could not get along without it. *Food is essential to man. Rungs are essential to a ladder. The pitcher and the catcher are essential parts of every baseball team. I couldn't put together this model car because an essential piece was missing. Good brakes are necessary on an automobile. Learning how to study is a necessary part of school. It is necessary to have fire drills often.*

Valuable means important because of being very useful or worth a lot. *She learned a valuable lesson when she had to write her whole paragraph over because no one could read it. An extra hour of practice is valuable to a musician. A hammer is a valuable tool to a carpenter. Valuable papers and jewels should be kept in a safe place. Valuable time was lost when we turned onto the wrong road.*

Look up GREAT and LARGE for other words you might want to use.

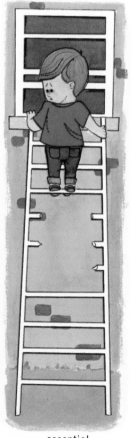

essential

ANTONYMS: unimportant, minor, trivial

IMPRISON	Look up SHUT.
IMPROPER	Look up antonyms of RIGHT.
IMPROVE	Look up HELP.
IMPURE	Look up DIRTY. Look up antonyms of CLEAN.
INAPPROPRIATE	Look up antonyms of RIGHT.
INCORRECT	Look up antonyms of RIGHT.
INDIFFERENT	Look up antonyms of EXCITED.
INJURE	Look up HURT.
INQUIRE	Look up ASK.
INSANE	Look up MAD.
INSTANT	Look up FAST (adj).
INSTANTLY	Look up FAST (adv).
INTELLIGENT	Look up SMART (adj).

imprison

INTERESTING

INTERESTING means holding your attention. Whatever holds your attention is not boring or dull. You can read an *interesting* book, hear an *interesting* story, take an *interesting* trip, or meet an *interesting* person. But many other words can be used to describe more precisely how *interesting* something is.

entertaining
amusing
fascinating
absorbing
exciting
thrilling

Entertaining describes someone or something that holds your attention in a pleasant and enjoyable way. A person who performs tricks or tells funny stories is *entertaining*. *Feeding time at the zoo was an entertaining sight. We spent an entertaining evening with our old friends.*

126

absorbing

Amusing means even more enjoyable than entertaining. An *amusing* book makes you laugh. You enjoy it so much you feel good even after you finish it. *My kitten playing with a string is an amusing sight. She read the class a very amusing poem.*

Fascinating means so interesting that it pulls your attention like a magnet. *The detective's solution of the mystery made a fascinating story. The magician did some fascinating tricks with a quarter and a dime.*

The word *absorb* means "soak up like a sponge," so *absorbing* means "soaking up your attention." A TV show may be so *absorbing* that you don't hear your mother call you to supper.

Exciting and *thrilling* mean interesting enough to make you feel happy or afraid or shivery or even angry. An *exciting* race will hold your attention. Riding on a roller coaster is *exciting*. A *thrilling* rescue or a *thrilling* end to a game may give you goose pimples. You may have an *exciting* argument over something. *A band playing "The Star Spangled Banner" can be thrilling to hear.*

ANTONYMS: uninteresting, boring, dull

INTRODUCE	Look up START. Look up antonyms of END (v).
INVENT	Look up MAKE and START.
IRRITABLE	Look up MAD.
IRRITATED	Look up MAD.
ISOLATED	Look up LONELY.

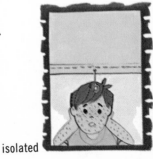

isolated

127

JAMMED	Look up FULL.
JAUNT	Look up TRIP.
JOG	Look up RUN.
JOLLY	Look up HAPPY.
JOURNEY	Look up TRIP.
JOYFUL	Look up HAPPY.
JUBILANT	Look up HAPPY.

JUMP

JUMP means throw oneself into the air. It also means leave the ground or a surface as if thrown into the air. *The cat **jumped** onto the table, but we made her **jump** off at once. The girls **jumped** up and down as they cheered the team to victory.*
But *jump* is often used differently, too. A train *jumps* the track if it goes off the rails. You say you *jump* when a sudden noise makes your body jerk—but you don't really leave the ground. You can win at checkers by *jumping* your opponent's kings. But you really move your king over his. To start

a race the starter shoots a gun. Anyone who runs before the shot is fired *"jumps* the gun." So if you begin something too soon, you *"jump* the gun."

spring
leap
bound
skip
hop
vault
hurdle
dive
plunge

Spring and *leap* mean jump. A cowboy may *spring* into the saddle. A boy can *leap* across a stream.

Bound and *skip* mean move quickly with many leaps. *The dog **bounded** into the room. The child **skipped** down the sidewalk. You can **skip** rope today.*

Hop means jump on one foot or jump with both feet together. If you drop a rock on your toe, you might *hop* around on the other foot. Some birds *hop* around on the ground looking for worms.

Vault means leap or spring or leap over something. You can *vault* a fence by putting your hands on it and swinging yourself over.

Hurdle means jump over something while running. *He **hurdled** a rope stretched across the road.*

Dive or *plunge* can mean jump or be thrown suddenly downward or into something, usually headfirst. You *dive* from a diving board into the pool. *The boy **dived** (or **dove**) twice to show me how.* You might run down the beach and *plunge* into the water.

Just as *jump* is used for other actions, some of its synonyms are used when you don't really mean *jump.* For example, if you pass over something—miss a line in a book you are reading, or turn some pages and begin to read further on—you have *skipped* a line or the pages. A person sometimes *hurdles* a problem if he faces it and overcomes or solves it. You may *plunge* into a hard job and get it done.

hop

JUST

Look up RIGHT.

KEEP

KEEP means hold on to. It's smart to **keep** part of your allowance. Some people **keep** shoes that are worn out. Other people discard them.

Keep also means take care of. You may **keep** goldfish or **keep** your neighbors' lawn or **keep** their dog when they go away.

Keep can also mean stay off or away from, or it can mean make someone or something stay off or away from. You **kept** off the grass in summer and **kept** the snow off the sidewalk in winter. Rain **has kept** you inside. You **keep** from falling.

save
preserve
conserve
tend
protect
guard
hold

Save, preserve, conserve, are other words for **keep.** Most people try to **save** money or **save** time. The government tries to **preserve** parts of this country and keep them as they were in the days of the Pilgrims. Travelers in a desert must **conserve** their supply of water. Nations **conserve** their forests. A swimmer must **conserve** his strength.

Tend means take care of something. You **tend** flowers that you have planted. A storekeeper **tends** his store.

protect

KEPT

KIND

sympathetic
helpful
thoughtful
considerate
gentle
pleasant
friendly
tactful

thoughtful

Protect and *guard* mean take care of and keep from harm or damage. An umbrella *protects* you from the rain. A watchdog *guards* a house.

Hold can mean keep from. If you *hold* your tongue, you keep from speaking. When soldiers *hold* their fire, they keep from shooting.

ANTONYMS: lose, let go, throw away, discard

KEPT is the past tense and past participle of KEEP.

A *kind* person is one who is interested in others. He is never cruel. A *kind* deed is one that helps someone. Many other words describe someone who is *kind* or something that shows kindness.

A *sympathetic* person listens to your troubles, understands your problems, and knows how you feel.

A *helpful* person will do anything he can to help you.

A person is *thoughtful* and *considerate* if he is careful of other people's feelings, and if he thinks about what others want and need, rather than only what he wants. Remembering someone's birthday is a *thoughtful* thing to do. Serving a guest's favorite food when he comes to dinner is *considerate.*

A *gentle* person is not rough or mean.

Pleasant and *friendly* describe people who are fun to be with and who are interested in you. A *pleasant* person is not ugly or quarrelsome.

Tactful means careful of another's feelings. A *tactful* person tries to correct someone's mistake without making him angry.

ANTONYMS: cold, mean, unpleasant, unkind, cruel, ugly

131

LAID   LAID is the past tense and past participle of LAY.

LARGE   LARGE is the opposite of <u>little</u> or <u>small</u>.

Large means bigger in size or amount than other
things like it—a *large* stone or a *large* bunch of grapes
or a *large* city. Like the word *big,* the word *large* is
used for many things of different sizes, and you
can't really tell what a person means when he calls
something *large* unless he is measuring its size against
something else like it. If, for example, he sees three
pieces of pie and says "I'll take the *large* one," then
you know what he means by *large.*

huge   *Huge* can mean having or containing a large amount
vast   of something. *An ocean is a **huge** body of water.*
immense   *I had a **huge** dish of ice cream.*
enormous   *Vast* means stretching over a large area. *A **vast***
giant   *desert stretched ahead of us.*
gigantic   *Immense* and *enormous* describe something
colossal   so large that the size can hardly be imagined. When
                you lie on the ground and look at the sky, it seems
                *immense. An **enormous** red moon came up over the lake.*

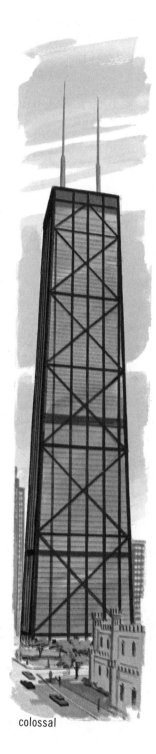

colossal

Giant and **gigantic** also mean very much larger than other objects. *The hunter saw one **giant** footprint in the snow. A **gigantic** tree towered above the others in the forest.*

Colossal usually describes something tremendously large that has been built by men. This word has an interesting history.

Many, many years ago there was an ancient city called Rhodes. The people of Rhodes wanted to do business with travelers from other countries, so they tried to think of some way to attract ships to their harbor. They found a sculptor who agreed to carve a gigantic statue of the sun god. He worked on the statue for many years, but at last it was finished. The people called the statue the Colossus of Rhodes. It was a hundred feet tall, and it stood in the harbor, facing out to sea. After many hundreds of years, the statue was destroyed by an earthquake. So today no one knows exactly what the Colossus looked like. But it has been said that the statue stood across the harbor with one foot on each side of it so the ships could pass beneath. In one hand the Colossus is supposed to have held a beacon to guide the sailors. Of course, such a sight did attract many ships, and Rhodes became an important city.

We still call a gigantic statue a *colossus*. We might refer to a huge man as a *colossus*. And a skyscraper or a bridge or anything made by man that is really large we may call **colossal.**

Look up GREAT and IMPORTANT for other words you might want to use.

ANTONYMS: small, tiny, fine, little

133

LAUGH

LAUGH means show joy or amusement or scorn by the look on your face and by making a certain sound. You can *laugh* at a joke or at an amusing sight. You can *laugh* at someone without being amused. Many words show different ways of laughing even though these words are not all synonyms.

smile
grin
chuckle
giggle
snicker
guffaw
howl
roar

Smile and *grin* are not the same as laugh, but you might consider them the weakest words for laugh.

When you *smile,* your eyes brighten, and the corners of your mouth turn up. When you *grin,* you smile but open your lips and show your teeth. By *smiling* or *grinning* you are able to show amusement or joy or scorn without making any sound at all.

You *chuckle* when you laugh very quietly. *Father chuckles sometimes as he reads the newspaper.*

You *giggle* when you keep catching your breath and making a continuous noise as you laugh. People sound foolish if they *giggle* a lot. Sometimes you *giggle* when you are nervous or embarrassed rather than when you are amused or happy.

You *snicker* if you laugh but try to cover it up. Sometimes children in class will *snicker* at something when they know they shouldn't.

When you *guffaw,* you just open your mouth and let out a great big laugh, usually about something that strikes you as very funny. This is one of the strongest words for laugh.

Howl and *roar* are ways in which animals make noise, but we often say people *howl* or *roar* with laughter.

smile

grin

giggle

guffaw

LAUGHABLE

Look up FUNNY.

134

LAUNCH	Look up START. Look up antonyms of END (v).
LAY	Look up PUT.
LEAD	Look up SHOW.

lead

LEAN	Look up THIN.
LEAP	Look up JUMP.
LEAPED	LEAPED is a past tense and past participle of LEAP.
LEAPT	LEAPT is a past tense and past participle of LEAP.
LEAVE	Look up GO. Look up antonyms of CARRY, of CHOOSE, of COME.
LED	LED is the past tense and past participle of LEAD.
LEFT	LEFT is the past tense and past participle of LEAVE.
LENIENT	Look up SOFT.
LET GO	Look up antonyms of CARRY, of CATCH, of KEEP.
LEVEL	Look up SMOOTH.
LIGHT	Look up BRIGHT. Look up antonyms of HARD.
LIGHTHEARTED	Look up HAPPY.

LIKE	LIKE means feel agreeable toward or pleased with. You may *like* your teacher or *like* candy or *like* swimming. It also means have a wish for something. Maybe you'd *like* to be a doctor when you grow up.

enjoy
be fond of
admire
want
love

Enjoy may be used if you speak of taking pleasure in something. *Be fond of* is used for something you like very much. You *enjoy* swimming or *enjoy* a good book. You probably wouldn't say you *are fond of* a good book. You could *be fond of* candy. You may *enjoy* eating, but you *are fond of* food.

You *admire* someone if you like what he has done or the kind of person he is. You might *admire* an excellent athlete or a courageous explorer. You might *admire* a beautiful object—but you can't always use *admire* for *like.* You may *admire* your teacher, but you wouldn't *admire* candy or swimming.

Want means desire very much or even need something. *Men want freedom. Everyone wants to be loved.*

Love is stronger than like. You *love* something or someone. But many people use it even for things they care just a little for, so *love* is a tired word. It's a good idea to use other words that tell more exactly how you feel, and save *love* for things and people that really mean the most to you.

ANTONYMS: dislike, hate, loathe

LIKING	Look up LOVE (n).
LIMIT	Look up END (n).
LIMP (v)	Look up WALK.
LIMP (adj)	Look up antonyms of HARD.

limp

136

LINGER	Look up antonyms of HURRY.

LITTLE

LITTLE is the opposite of big or large.
Little means less than other things in size or
amount or value. *The **little** bear was not as big as the
other two bears. You may eat a **little** candy when
you'd like to eat a lot.*

small
tiny
fine
scanty
skimpy
outgrown

You can use *small* and *tiny* instead of *little*
when you are talking about the size of some object.
You might speak of a *small* child or a *tiny* child.
You wouldn't use *small* or *tiny* if you were talking
about the amount of something. A little candy usually
means a few pieces of candy. A *small* or *tiny*
candy would mean one piece that was very little.
If you ask for a little milk, you mean a *small* amount.
You wouldn't say a *small* or *tiny* milk. You'd have
to say a *small* glass of milk or a *tiny* bit of milk.

Fine can mean small. Print that is so small
you can hardly read the words is called *fine* print.
Something that is ground into very small pieces
may be called *fine*—*fine* sugar or *fine* sand.

Scanty, skimpy, and *outgrown* are not synonyms of
little, but they are good words to describe
something that is too little or not quite enough. You
might have a *scanty* breakfast if you did not have
nearly as much as you wanted. A dress or slacks that
fit but that have no extra material at the hem so
they can be lengthened can be called *skimpy.* You
write a *skimpy* book report if you don't tell enough
for anyone else to know what the book is about.

Outgrown is a good word to use for clothes
that are too little because you are getting bigger.

ANTONYMS: big, large, bulky, great, huge

outgrown

137

LOADED	Look up FULL.
LOATHE	Look up HATE.
	Look up antonyms of LIKE.
LOCATE	Look up FIND.
LOITER	Look up antonyms of HURRY.

loaded

LONELY

LONELY means being away from others. *Lonely* and all the synonyms below can describe how a person feels or how something looks. When *lonely* is used to describe people, it usually means feeling sad because of being away from friends or family. A *lonely* child sitting on a curb probably does wish for company. But when you speak of one *lonely* tree high on a hill, you don't mean the tree is feeling sad. You mean that it is the only tree there. A *lonely* road is not sad, but it is without houses or much traffic.

alone
lonesome
forlorn
isolated
desolate

Alone means being away from others or being the only one of its kind. It does not mean feeling sad. A person who lives *alone* may not be lonely. *Alone* is a word like *afraid*. You can say "*The man was alone in the room*," but you can't say "*The alone man was in the room*."

Lonesome usually does mean sad because you are lonely. You may be *lonesome* for a friend.

Forlorn is stronger than lonesome.
If you are all alone in a crowd, you may be *forlorn*. You are not away from others, but you feel lonely. *The little girl looked forlorn as she waved good-by.*

Isolated means cut off or set apart from others. A cabin by itself in the mountains is *isolated*. A boy with measles is *isolated* from his friends.

lonely

Desolate means very, very lonely and away from others. If you have lost a friend, you may be *desolate.* A farm miles away from a town may be a *desolate* place, even though people live there.

LONESOME	Look up LONELY.
LOOK	LOOK and *see* mean almost the same thing. *Look* or *look at* means take in or understand something by using the eyes. To *look,* you focus your eyes on something. *See* means take in the sight of something. You *see* a movie. When you are *looking at* one thing, you are also able to *see* what is on both sides of it. You can *see* daylight without *looking at* it. *She looked at the sky and saw millions of stars.* There are many other words that describe how people *look* or *look at* or *see.*

see	*Behold, observe, view,* all can be used instead
behold	of *look at. Behold* is often used when
observe	attention is being called to something. *Observe*
view	means look at closely and carefully. (*Observe*
glance	can also mean say.) A magician may say,
gaze	*"Behold* an empty hat." Then, as you look at
stare	it, he pulls a rabbit out. He may say,
glare	*"Observe* the coin in my hand." As you look at
peer	it, he makes it disappear. You may *behold* a lofty
peek	mountain. You also *view* a sunset or magnificent
watch	sight when you look at it. You *observe* something
examine	by looking at it with close attention. If you *observe* how your mother bakes a cake, you may be able to bake one yourself. People

TURN THE PAGE TURN THE PAGE TURN THE PAGE TURN THE PAGE TURN TH

gaze

stare

glare

peek

examine

observe the movements of birds by looking through field glasses. You *view* television. You wouldn't *observe* it or *behold* it.

You *glance* at something when you look at it just for a moment. *He* **glanced** *out the window as he passed. She* **glanced** *at me, then turned away.*

You *gaze* when you look for a long time. You may *gaze* at a bee on a flower, watching it get the nectar. You may *gaze* out the window, looking at nothing.

If you *stare* at something, you look a long time at it, perhaps without blinking your eyes. *We* **stared** *at the boy because we couldn't believe what he was saying. Most people think it is impolite to* **stare.**

If someone *glares* at you, he looks at you angrily. *The bus driver* **glared** *at us for shouting. When I came home late, my father* **glared.**

Peer means look sharply and curiously. *The old lady* **peered** *at us through her glasses. He* **peered** *down into the hole.*

You *peek* at something secretly or from a hiding place. *We* **peeked** *at the presents on the shelf. They* **peeked** *through a hole in the fence.*

Watch means look at or observe for a long time in order to follow the movement of something or in order to be ready for something. You may *watch* a ball game. You can *watch* the sun go down or *watch* the cat so that it doesn't claw the furniture.

You *examine* something if you look at it or look it over very carefully and completely. *The umpire* **examined** *the ball before he threw it. The dog* **examined** *the bone before he began to chew on it. The doctor* **examined** *my throat.*

140

LOOM	Look up COME.
LOPE	Look up RUN.
LOSE	Look up antonyms of GET, of FIND, of KEEP.
LOST	LOST is the past tense and past participle of LOSE.
LOUD	LOUD is the opposite of quiet and soft. **Loud** means having or making a big sound. You may hear a **loud** noise or speak in a **loud** voice or drop a book with a **loud** bang. **Loud** also means very bright in color. *The man wore a **loud** necktie.*

noisy
shrill
boisterous
thunderous
roaring
showy

Noisy describes a lot of loud, harsh sounds. Boys and girls can have a **noisy** game of tag or a quiet game of checkers. A classroom may be **noisy** before the bell rings, but it becomes quiet when school begins. A lot of traffic on a street is **noisy**.

Shrill means having or making a loud, high, sharp sound. The sound of a whistle is **shrill**. When children play, their voices may grow **shrill**. A soft voice is the opposite of a **shrill** or loud one.

Boisterous means loud and noisy. *The **boisterous** children outside shouted. When they went inside, they spoke in subdued voices.*

Thunderous describes a loud noise that sounds like thunder. *The actors received **thunderous** applause.* A big waterfall sounds **thunderous**. It is never still. A long, loud, deep sound is **roaring**. *The **roaring** fire was hard to put out. **Roaring** planes flew low.*

Showy means too bright or loud. Someone who wants to show how rich he is might buy a **showy** car. Also see BRIGHT for other words.

shrill

ANTONYMS: quiet (adj), soft, still, silent, subdued

LOVE (v)   Look up LIKE.
                            Look up antonyms of HATE.

LOVE (n)   LOVE is a strong feeling of being drawn to a person
                            or to an object. You may feel *love* for someone if
                            you admire and enjoy being with that person and
                            want to do anything you can to make the person happy.
                            Love of an object is a desire to have or enjoy it
                            because it is beautiful or is delightful to you or
                            seems necessary for your happiness.

           affection   *Affection* is a kind, warm feeling for someone or
           devotion   something. It is not as strong as love. You may feel
           friendship   *love* for your own mother and *affection* for your
           fondness   friend's mother.
           liking   *Devotion* is a very strong feeling of love sometimes for
                            a person but often for something you believe in. A
                            patriot feels *devotion to* his country. A soldier has
                            devotion to duty. Many people have *devotion to* God.
                            Friendship is a strong feeling of affection and
                            trust and enjoyment two or more persons have
                            for each other. Children form many *friendships*
                            when they go to school.
                            Fondness and *liking* are feelings of enjoyment and
                            sometimes affection for things and animals. Some
                            people have a *fondness* for cats. You may have a
                            liking for peanut butter or a *fondness* for hiking in
                            the woods. You would use *for* after the words
                            affection, fondness, friendship, liking. You would
                            use *to* after the word *devotion. For* and *of* may both
                            follow *love.* You may feel *love for* someone
                            and *love of* something.

142

LOVELY

LOVELY is a tired word. It is used many times instead of some words that might describe more precisely what you are talking about.

Lovely is a synonym for BEAUTIFUL, but before you use it, why not look up some of these words?

When you speak of a *lovely* picture, you might mean *beautiful* or *pleasing* or *attractive*.

A *lovely* day is probably *sunny* or *cool* or *warm* or *clear* or *mild*.

A *lovely* child is *attractive, good, pretty, pleasant, happy, interesting, friendly,* perhaps *naughty* at times, and *comical*.

A *lovely* time might be *delightful* or *interesting, happy, quiet, peaceful,* or *exciting* or *hilarious*.

A *lovely* house could be *attractive, pleasant, beautiful, comfortable, cheerful, warm,* and *peaceful*.

A *lovely* view is usually *magnificent, wonderful, delightful, thrilling,* or *hushed, calm, peaceful*.

A *lovely* friend is *sympathetic, kind, considerate,* perhaps *amusing,* always *interesting*.

A *lovely* party could be *delightful, exciting, gay, pleasant, enjoyable, jolly*.

A *lovely* book can be *exciting, delightful, interesting, funny, sad, scary, pleasing, beautiful*.

LUDICROUS   Look up FUNNY.

LURCH   Look up WALK.

LURE   Look up PULL.

lure

MAD

crazy
insane
angry
annoyed
irritated
exasperated
disgusted
disgruntled
enraged
furious
fit to be tied
cranky
grouchy
cross
irritable
ornery
disagreeable

MAD means without sense or self-control. A *mad* person may be *crazy* or *insane.*

A *crazy* or *insane* person does not always know what he is doing. But *mad* is often used to mean *angry*—greatly displeased about something. A person may be *angry* because something has made him so. Some people seem always to be *angry* about something or about nothing or about life in general.

Here are words to describe someone who is not *angry* all the time, but is displeased once in a while.

Annoyed, irritated, exasperated, mean bothered by something. *The lady seemed annoyed because I had dialed the wrong number. The second time, she seemed irritated. The third time I dialed the wrong number, she was exasperated.*

Disgusted means turning away from something unpleasant or sickening. *Many disgusted people walked out of the theater after waiting an hour for the show to begin. We felt disgusted when we saw how dirty the kitchen was.*

annoyed

irritated

exasperated

fit to be tied

Disgruntled describes someone who is in a bad mood because of something that has happened. *The owner of the store tried to please a **disgruntled** customer by giving back his money.*

Enraged and ***furious*** mean filled with rage or fury. *An **enraged** lion tried to claw its trainer. The **furious** girl slammed her book shut and threw it down on the table.*

Fit to be tied is a phrase for someone who is very angry. *When Dad couldn't find his fishing rod that I had borrowed, he was **fit to be tied**. The fourth time I dialed the wrong number, the lady who answered was **fit to be tied**.*

Cranky, grouchy, and ***cross*** describe people who feel angry most of the time. A ***cranky*** person becomes angry very easily, grumbles about everything, and is not pleasant to be with. A ***grouchy*** person complains about everything and doesn't try to get along with others. A person may be ***cross*** and speak sharply if he is not feeling well or if something doesn't please him. *The baby is **cross** when she is sleepy. Mother will be **cross** if I don't make my bed.*

Irritable and ***ornery*** describe people who are almost always angry or who get angry very easily. Sometimes the smallest thing will upset an ***irritable*** person. An ***ornery*** man will do the opposite of whatever anyone wants him to do.

Disagreeable means not willing to go along with someone else's ideas or plans. A ***disagreeable*** person is very hard to get along with.

ANTONYMS: calm (adj), unruffled, pleasant, patient, peaceful, placid

145

MADE	MADE is the past tense and past participle of MAKE.
MAGNIFICENT	Look up GREAT.
MAIL	Look up SEND.
MAJESTIC	Look up GREAT.

mail

MAKE

create
invent
establish
set up
originate
build
construct
assemble
manufacture
put together
fashion
form
shape
cause
force
compel

MAKE is used in many ways. It always means bring something into being or bring something to pass. You *make* mud pies. Perhaps you *made* a cake yesterday. Automobiles *have made* travel easier.

Create and *invent* mean make something new or different from anything else. An artist may *create* a beautiful painting. A musician may *create* a great piece of music. A cook may *create* a new kind of dessert. Many people *have invented* machines that make life easier.

Establish and *set up* mean make or start something for the first time. People *establish* or *set up* rules for a new game or laws for a country. They *establish* schools and churches. Rich men often *set up* or *establish* funds of money to help others.

Originate is used for starting a new idea or a new way of doing something. *The Pilgrims* *originated* Thanksgiving Day.

Build and *construct* mean make something from materials and according to a plan. Carpenters *build* or *construct* houses from brick and wood. Men in museums *construct* models of dinosaurs.

Build up can mean put something together over a long period of time. You *build up* a bank account by saving a little money each week and putting it in the bank.

Assemble, manufacture, and *put together* mean make an object by fitting parts where they belong. Many people *assemble* or *put together* radios and toys and furniture from hobby kits. Companies *manufacture* radios and toys by using machines that make all the parts and then *put* them *together.* It's fun to *put together* a banana split.

Fashion and *form* mean make in a certain pattern or outline. These words are often used when something is made by hand. *Fashion* may be used when someone creates one object out of another or out of unusual material. You can *fashion* a lamp out of an old bottle. A shipwrecked sailor may *fashion* a sail from his shirt. You can *form* a plan of action or *form* a circle on the playground.

Shape usually means give a certain form to something. Children might *form* a snowman out of snow. But they would *shape* snow into a snowman.

Cause means make something happen or make someone do something. *Rain caused the accident. Sickness caused his absence from school.* You could say the storm *made* you late, but you would have to say the storm *caused* you *to be* late.

Force and *compel* mean use power to make something happen or someone act. *The door was locked, but he forced it open. The farmer forced the sheep to go through the gate one by one. The storm compelled us to go inside. The game was so exciting we were compelled to watch it.*

See START for other good words.

ANTONYMS: break, demolish, tear down, wreck, destroy

fashion

147

MANUFACTURE	Look up MAKE.
MAR	Look up HURT.
MARCH	Look up WALK.
MARVELOUS	Look up WONDERFUL.
MASK	Look up HIDE. Look up antonyms of SHOW.

mar

MEAN	Look up antonyms of GREAT and of KIND.
MELANCHOLY	Look up SAD. Look up antonyms of HAPPY.
MELT	Look up GO.
MEND	Look up antonyms of BREAK.
MERRY	Look up HAPPY. Look up antonyms of SAD.
MIGHTY	Look up GREAT.

melt

MILD	Look up SOFT. Look up antonyms of HARD and of HOT.
MINOR	Look up antonyms of IMPORTANT.
MISERABLE	Look up SAD. Look up antonyms of HAPPY.
MISLEAD	Look up GYP.
MISLED	MISLED is the past tense and past participle of MISLEAD.

MISPLACE	Look up antonyms of FIND.
MISS	Look up antonyms of CATCH.
MISTAKEN	Look up antonyms of RIGHT.

miss

148

MISTY	Look up DIM.
MODERN	Look up antonyms of OLD.
MOIST	Look up WET.
MOTIONLESS	Look up QUIET (adj).
MOURNFUL	Look up SAD.
	Look up antonyms of HAPPY.

MOVE

MOVE is a word that has many meanings.
Move means change from one position to another
or go from one place to another. Everything that lives
moves. It grows or changes and becomes something
else. You can *move.* You can *move* something.
You can *move* somebody. You *move* when you stand
up or sit down. You might *move* to another town.
You can *move* your finger or your eyes. You can
move a baby from its bed to your lap. Every kind
of creature can *move.* So can things. A train or ship
or a wave or a rock can *move* or *be moved.*
A driver can *move* an auto or a horse. At the same
time he is making them *move.*

Entry words in this book that mean *move* in some
way are COME and GO, WALK and RUN, FLY and
FALL, PULL and PUSH, START, STOP, SHUT and
HURRY, JUMP, PUT, CARRY, SEND, THROW.

You can think of many more words for *move*
that are not all in this book. Fish *swim,*
worms *crawl,* frogs *hop,* mice *scurry,* snakes *slither,*
wheels *roll,* skis *slide,* boats *float.*
They all *move.*

MUFFLED	Look up DIM.

NARROW	Look up THIN.
NAUGHTY	Look up BAD.
NEARLY	Look up ABOUT.
NEAT	Look up CLEAN.
NECESSARY	Look up IMPORTANT.
NEIGHBOR	Look up FRIEND.
NET	Look up CATCH.

net

NEW	Look up antonyms of OLD.
NIBBLE	Look up EAT.
NICE	NICE is a tired word that is often used instead of one that tells more exactly what you mean. Why not look up some different ones and try them next time you start to use *nice?*
	A *nice* day or *nice* weather is *pleasant* or *beautiful, mild* or *sunny, warm* or *cool, magnificent, quiet.*
	A *nice* person may be *friendly, attractive, beautiful, pleasant, kind, interesting, amusing, comical, quiet, patient, smart, neat.*
	A *nice* time could be *happy, pleasant, peaceful, delightful, amusing, gay, exciting.*
	A *nice* dress or sweater is probably *pretty, bright, attractive, neat, appropriate, silky, soft.*
NOBLE	Look up GREAT.
NOISE	NOISE is something almost everyone knows.

noise

Turn

There are many degrees or amounts of noise. Here are some good words for them.

racket
ruckus
din
flurry
commotion
hubbub
clamor
uproar
bedlam

Racket is a clattering noise. A carpenter driving nails or a plumber pounding on pipes can make a **racket**. *The boys made a great **racket** when they raced down the stairs with their football shoes on.*

Ruckus is noisy talk or a noisy quarrel. One loud talker can cause a **ruckus**. People who quarrel over something raise their voices and get excited enough to start a **ruckus**. *Two boys started a **ruckus** over who should go first.*

Din is a mixture of loud, confused noises. It is a racket that may last a long time. Sometimes when you are eating in a cafeteria, it is hard to hear what the person across the table is saying because of the **din** made by dishes clattering and people talking. Traffic often makes a **din.**

Flurry is a sudden short, noisy movement that breaks into a quiet place or group of people. You might cause a **flurry** if you forgot where you were and began to whistle in the library. *The bridegroom caused a **flurry** when he dropped the ring.*

flurry

racket

Commotion means a mixture of noise and movement. It is louder and bigger than a flurry. *There was a **commotion** in the hall when two men started shouting at the speaker.*

Hubbub means loud, confused sounds or noises. It may be louder than a din. *The **hubbub** was deafening when everyone talked at once.*

Clamor is a loud noise, made by people or animals, that lasts a long time. Often a *clamor* is raised by people or animals who want something or are angry. *The animals in their cages set up a **clamor** at feeding time. The speaker could not be heard above the angry **clamor** of the crowd.*

Uproar is probably the loudest noise. An *uproar* can start as a ruckus or a commotion, then grow as more people or animals join in. *The city was in an **uproar** when the mayor resigned.*

Bedlam is an interesting word for a place that is filled with noise and confusion.

There once was an insane asylum in London called the Hospital of St. Mary of Bethlehem. Its long name gradually became shortened to Bedlam. The insane people made so much noise with their wild howls and shrieks that *bedlam* became a word for any noisy, confused scene or place. *When I opened the door, the room was a **bedlam**.*

ANTONYMS: quiet (n), stillness

NOISY	Look up LOUD. Look up antonyms of QUIET (adj).
NUDGE	Look up PUSH.
NUMB	Look up QUIET (adj).

OBSERVE	Look up LOOK and SAY.
OBSOLETE	Look up OLD.
OBSTRUCT	Look up antonyms of HELP.
OBTAIN	Look up GET.
OCCUPIED	Look up antonyms of EMPTY.
ODD	Look up QUEER.

OLD   OLD describes something or someone that has lived for a long time or that existed long ago. *Old* is like the word *big.* It describes anything older than something else. If you buy a new pencil, the one you had yesterday is *old.* Your uncle may be *old,* but not as *old* as your grandfather. New and young are both antonyms of *old.*

ancient   *Ancient* means very old or happening long ago.
olden   Cavemen lived in *ancient* times. Museums
aged   preserve *ancient* tools.
elderly
antique   *Olden* is often used by poets and storytellers. *The*
obsolete   *olden days were long ago.* The Romans and the Pilgrims lived in *olden* days, but this does not mean they lived at the same time.

154

A very old person is sometimes called *aged* or
elderly. Some people have *aged* grandparents.
Antique means very old but still existing and still used.
Many people use *antique* tables, chests, and chairs
in their homes.

Obsolete means old and no longer used. Steam
engines were used to pull trains, but now diesel
engines are used, so steam engines are *obsolete.*
Years ago milk was delivered by horse and wagon.
Now trucks have made milk wagons *obsolete.*

ANTONYMS: new, modern, young

OLDEN	Look up OLD.
OPEN	Look up START.
	Look up antonyms of END (v) and of SHUT.
OPERATE	Look up RUN and WORK.
OPPOSE	Look up FIGHT.
	Look up antonyms of HELP.
ORDINARY	Look up antonyms of WONDERFUL and of QUEER.
ORIGINATE	Look up MAKE and START.
ORNERY	Look up MAD.
OUTCOME	Look up END (n).
OUTGROWN	Look up LITTLE.
OUTING	Look up TRIP.
OUTLANDISH	Look up QUEER.
OUTSET	Look up antonyms of END (n).
OVERFLOWING	Look up FULL.

open

PACKED	Look up antonyms of EMPTY.
PAL	Look up FRIEND.
PARCHED	Look up antonyms of WET.
PASS	Look up THROW.
PATIENT	Look up antonyms of MAD.
PAUSE	Look up STOP.
PEACEFUL	Look up QUIET (adj). Look up antonyms of MAD.
PECULIAR	Look up QUEER.
PEEK	Look up LOOK.
PEEL	Look up CUT.
PEER	Look up LOOK.
PEPPERY	Look up HOT.
PETTY	Look up antonyms of GREAT.
PICK	Look up CHOOSE.
PITCH	Look up THROW.

pitch

PLACE	Look up PUT.
PLACID	Look up antonyms of MAD.
PLAIN	Look up antonyms of BEAUTIFUL and of WONDERFUL.
PLAN	Look up THINK.
PLEASANT	Look up WONDERFUL, GOOD, and KIND. Look up antonyms of MAD.
PLUMP	Look up antonyms of THIN.
PLUNGE	Look up JUMP and PUSH.
POINT OUT	Look up SHOW.
POKY	Look up antonyms of FAST (adj).
POLISHED	Look up SMOOTH.
POLLUTED	Look up DIRTY. Look up antonyms of CLEAN.
PONDER	Look up THINK.
POOR	Look up BAD.
POWERFUL	Look up STRONG.
PRACTICALLY	Look up ABOUT.
PRECARIOUS	Look up DANGEROUS.
PRESENT	Look up SHOW.
PRESERVE	Look up KEEP.
PRETTY	Look up BEAUTIFUL.
PREVENT	Look up STOP.
PROBLEM	Look up antonyms of ANSWER (n).

place

poky

powerful

PROCEED	Look up GO.
PROD	Look up PUSH.
PROGRESS	Look up GO.
PROPEL	Look up PUSH.
PROPER	Look up RIGHT.
PROTECT	Look up KEEP.
PROVE	Look up SHOW.
PULL	PULL means make an object move toward or after you. It is the opposite of push. A dentist **pulls** teeth. A tractor **pulls** a plow.

draw
drag
haul

Draw means pull with a steady motion and without using much strength. A knight **draws** his sword. *You **drew** the curtains by pulling a cord.*

tow
tug
stretch
strain
attract
lure

Drag means pull something along the ground. You might **drag** a heavy chair across a thick carpet if you couldn't lift it, or **drag** a log up a hill to the campfire. You might have to **drag** your dog out of the house if it is cold and rainy and he doesn't want to go.

drag

tug

attract

If you *haul* something big or heavy, you pull it for a long distance. Trucks *haul* coal or iron bars or furniture. Freight trains *haul* many things.

You *tow* something when you pull it along behind a car or boat or whatever you are riding in. Tugboats *tow* larger boats up a river. Trucks and cars often *tow* trailers.

You *tug* if you pull hard, sometimes stopping to rest between pulls. You may *tug* at a door that is stuck and won't open. It might not open no matter how long you *tug* at it.

Stretch and *strain* can mean pull hard, too. If you *stretch* a rope from one tree to another, you pull it as tight as it will go. A dog that is tied up may *strain* at its leash trying to get away.

Attract and *lure* mean pull in a different way. Something *attracts* or *lures* by making you want to move toward it—by promising something good or interesting or exciting. A colorful cover can *attract* your attention to a book. Music may *attract* you to a merry-go-round. A cake *attracts* flies and draws them to it.
Sometimes the thing that *lures* is dangerous. A worm may *lure* fish to a fishhook. Cheese often *lures* a mouse into a trap.

Pull is used in many idioms.

If you get a fit of giggling in church or in class, you "*pull* yourself together" and stop.

If someone tells you a wild story just to tease you, she "*is pulling* your leg."

ANTONYMS: push, reject

159

PURE	Look up CLEAN.
	Look up antonyms of DIRTY.
PURPOSE	Look up END (n).
PUSH	PUSH means move yourself or move something ahead or aside or backward by force. It is the opposite of <u>pull</u>. You have to **push** aside the bushes and **push** through undergrowth if you are walking in the woods. You **push** back your dog if he jumps on you with muddy feet. In a crowded bus, you usually have to **push** your way past people who won't move. It is unpleasant **to be pushed** by someone behind you in a line.
shove *propel* *drive* *nudge* *thrust* *plunge* *encourage* *prod*	**Shove** means push roughly or carelessly. In a crowded street someone may **shove** you off the sidewalk. **Shove** also means push along on a surface. A baby may **shove** his dish off the table. You can **shove** something that is too heavy to lift. **Propel** means make something go forward. Rockets **propel** a spaceship by pushing it through the air. The propeller on a boat **propels** it by pushing it through the water. You can **propel** a log or a raft in the water by holding on to it and kicking your feet as you would if you were swimming.

propel

160

drive

drive

Drive means push or force on or forward. It can also mean make an object or an animal move or do something. A carpenter *drives* nails. A farmer *drives* his team or a tractor. Cowboys *drive* cattle.

Nudge means push gently. You might *nudge* a friend with your elbow to get his attention.

Thrust and *plunge* are good words to use when you mean push hard, and usually push into something. You *thrust* a knife into a watermelon to cut it open, or *thrust* a shovel into the ground when you dig a hole. You could *thrust* or *plunge* your hand into a pail of water or into a snowdrift to get something you've dropped or lost. Swimmers *plunge* into the water.

Encourage means push in a different way. You don't really push someone, but you coax and help and make him want to do something.

Prod is often used to mean make someone do something. It is stronger than encourage. Some people have to be constantly *prodded* into doing their homework or cleaning up their rooms.

ANTONYM: <u>pull</u>

161

PUT

PUT is a word that is used for many things. It really means move something to some place and leave it there. You **put** flowers **in** a vase and **put** the vase **on** the table. Perhaps you **put** fresh flowers there yesterday, too, or **have put** them there every day all summer. But you can **put away** your coat or you can **put** it **on**. Some people **put on** airs. A boss **puts** his men **to** work. A musician can **put** words **to** music. Some people **put** the blame for what they do **on** others. There are other words to use for **put** that have more precise meanings.

place
lay
set
deposit
arrange
spread

Place means put in a certain position. You **place** flowers in the middle of the table, or **place** chairs on each side of the table. You might **place** a heavy dish very carefully on the shelf.

Lay means put in a horizontal or lying-down position. You would **lay** your coat on a chair or **lay** the baby in its crib or **lay** a rug on the floor. You always have to **lay** something somewhere. You can **lay** yourself down, but you wouldn't usually say that. You would always use the verb *lie* for people or things that *are lying* down. *Your coat is lying on the chair. The baby lies in its crib.*

lay

162

Set means put in a certain position for a certain purpose. You **have set** the table when you have put food and dishes on it. *You set the baby in his highchair when his supper was ready.* The doctor **sets** a broken bone. A gardener **sets out** plants in the yard.

Deposit means put away—you **deposit** money in the bank. It also means put down or drop. A heavy rain may wash sand from a hill and **deposit** it on the sidewalk.

Arrange means put in some order. Library books **are arranged** on the shelves in a certain way. People **arrange** flowers in a vase.

Spread can be used to mean put something over or on top of something. You **spread** jelly on a piece of bread. At the beach people often **have spread** a blanket or towel to sit on. *Gardeners spread black dirt over our lawn last fall.*

ANTONYMS: take away, remove

PUT TOGETHER   Look up MAKE.

put together

QUAINT   Look up QUEER.

QUARREL   Look up FIGHT and TALK.

QUEER   QUEER means not <u>common</u>, or different in some
               way from <u>common</u>, everyday things. *The girl wore
               a **queer** costume to our party. Did you ever see
               such a **queer** hat? My voice sounded so **queer** over the
               telephone that Mother didn't recognize it.*

odd   **Odd** means different from what is expected or
unusual   planned. *I saw an **odd** sight on the way to school.
strange   The book had an **odd** ending.*
peculiar   **Unusual** means different from the usual or ordinary.
outlandish   *It was **unusual** for the old man to be out so early.*
quaint   **Strange** means odd and hard to understand or
weird   explain. *He heard a **strange** noise.*

               Peculiar describes the looks or actions of a person
               which are different from everyone else's. You can
               say someone has a **peculiar** walk, or that kind
               of walk is **peculiar** to him.

               Outlandish means something is so odd that it seems
               to have come from a different land. In ancient times,

164

before people traveled very much, any stranger from a foreign country who spoke or dressed differently was an "outlander." So something very odd or unusual is still called **outlandish**.

Quaint means odd or different because it is old-fashioned or out of style, though it may be pretty or attractive or pleasing. A **quaint** street is interesting to walk along.

quaint

Weird describes something so queer it can only be explained by supernatural or unearthly causes. We often use **weird** now to describe anything odd or hard to understand. *We saw some **weird** paintings at the museum.*

Look up FUNNY for other words to use.

ANTONYMS: common, regular, ordinary

QUESTION (v)	Look up antonyms of ANSWER (v).
QUESTION (n)	Look up antonyms of ANSWER (n).
QUIBBLE	Look up FIGHT.
QUICK	Look up FAST (adj).
QUICKLY	Look up FAST (adv).
QUICK-WITTED	Look up SMART (adj).

QUIET (adj)

QUIET is the opposite of <u>loud</u>. **Quiet** also means without much movement. A sleeping kitten is **quiet.** A dog that is usually **quiet** may become <u>restless</u> during a thunderstorm. *The house seemed **quiet** after the <u>boisterous</u> children went outside. The family spent a **quiet** day at home. Mother always speaks in a **quiet** voice when she tells my sister and me a secret.*

silent
still
calm
peaceful
soundless
speechless
dumb
shy
tame
subdued
motionless
numb

Silent is a very strong word for quiet. It means without any noise. *The children were **silent** as they waited for the results of the play tryouts. She looked at the **silent** telephone, wishing it would ring.*

Still, calm, and **peaceful** describe a gentle or hushed type of quiet. Wiggly children are often asked to be **still.** Trees are **still** when no wind moves their leaves. On a hot summer day the lake is usually **calm.** You would speak in a **calm** voice to a child who is lost. *The country is more **peaceful** than the busy city. Dad hopes to enjoy a **peaceful** evening when he sits down to read.*

Soundless describes a complete lack of noise. There probably isn't a **soundless** way to eat potato chips since they're so <u>noisy</u> when you bite them. A car with the motor turned off may be **soundless.**

Speechless and **dumb** mean not being able to speak. Many people use **dumb** as a synonym for **stupid,** but its first meaning is **speechless.** You would probably be **speechless** if you saw an elephant at a drinking fountain. All animals are **dumb**—except, perhaps, some parrots and parakeets. If something shocked or surprised you so much you couldn't say a word, it struck you **dumb.**

Shy means quiet and timid or easily frightened. *The new girl in our class is **shy**. Animals in the woods are **shy** and frightened of human beings.*

Tame describes a creature that has been trained to be obedient or gentle. *It would be fun to ride a **tame** elephant. The **tame** rabbits were eating sunflower seeds out of our hands.* **Tame** is the opposite of wild.

tame

Subdued means not loud or bold. *The boys were noisy outside, but in class they spoke in **subdued** voices.* Soft shades of tan, green, and yellow are called **subdued** colors because they are not too bright and loud. ***Motionless*** and ***numb*** mean without moving or unable to move. On a very cold day, you might discover that you had **numb** fingers and toes. *The **motionless** fisherman waited for a fish to bite.*

Antonyms: loud, boisterous, noisy, excited, restless, wild

QUIET (n)   Look up antonyms of NOISE.

QUIT   Look up STOP. QUIT is the same in the past tense and in the past-participle form.

R

RACE	Look up RUN.
RACKET	Look up NOISE.
RADIANT	Look up antonyms of DIM.
RAGGED	Look up ROUGH.
RAINY	Look up WET.
RAMBLE (v)	Look up GO.
RAMBLE (n)	Look up TRIP.
RAN	RAN is the past tense of RUN.
RAPID	Look up FAST (adj).
RAPIDLY	Look up FAST (adv).
RECEIVE	Look up GET. Look up antonyms of SEND.
RECKLESS	Look up CARELESS.
REFUSE	Look up antonyms of ASK and of CHOOSE.
REGULAR	Look up antonyms of QUEER.
REJECT	Look up antonyms of CHOOSE and of PULL.

ragged

RELINQUISH	Look up antonyms of GET.
REMAIN	Look up antonyms of RUN and of GO.
REMARK	Look up SAY.
REMOVE	Look up antonyms of PUT.
REPAIR	Look up antonyms of BREAK.

repair

REPLY (v)	Look up ANSWER (v).
	Look up antonyms of ASK.
REPLY (n)	Look up ANSWER (n).
REQUEST	Look up ASK.
RESPOND	Look up ANSWER (v).
	Look up antonyms of ASK.
RESPONSE	Look up ANSWER (n).
RESTLESS	Look up antonyms of QUIET (adj).
RESULT	Look up END (n).
RETORT (v)	Look up ANSWER (v).
RETORT (n)	Look up ANSWER (n).
RETREAT	Look up GO.
REVEAL	Look up SHOW.
	Look up antonyms of HIDE.
RIDICULOUS	Look up FUNNY.

RIGHT

RIGHT is the opposite of wrong. When something is free from any mistake or fault, you might say it is **right.** Usually something is **right** according to certain rules or standards. *Jim did the **right** thing when he apologized to his sister. But he had been wrong to hit her. When the teacher asked a question, Beth gave the **right** answer. Everyone must wear the **right** kind of shoes for gym.*

correct
fair
just
proper
appropriate

Correct means right or true or acceptable. *He used **correct** English in his theme, but his facts were incorrect. After two false starts, we found the **correct** way to put up the tent.*

Something right or honest according to reason or a set of rules is **fair** or **just.** *The judge tried to be **fair** to everyone. We think he made a **just** decision. It is **fair** for every player to have his turn. A law that is not **fair** to everyone is unjust.*

If something is especially right for the time or place, it is **proper** or **appropriate.** *The girl's clothes were **proper** for gardening. He knows the **proper** way to act at the dinner table. It is improper to talk with your mouth full. Heavy boots are **appropriate** to wear for skiing. High heels are inappropriate for little girls.* Wearing scuba gear to the dinner table would not be **appropriate.** In fact, it would not even be smart if you were very hungry! *It was **proper** for him to give a speech when he received the prize.*

Look up GOOD for other words you might like to use instead.

ANTONYMS: incorrect, false, improper, inappropriate, wrong, unjust, mistaken

RIGID   Look up HARD.

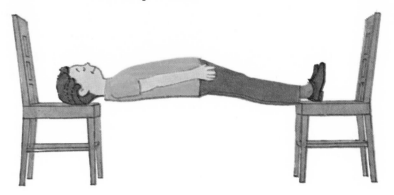

rigid

RISE   Look up START.
               Look up antonyms of FALL.

RISEN   RISEN is the past participle of RISE.

RISKY   Look up DANGEROUS.

ROAR   Look up LAUGH and SAY.

ROARING   Look up LOUD.

ROCKY   Look up ROUGH.

ROPE   Look up CATCH.

rope

ROSE   ROSE is the past tense of RISE.

ROUGH

ROUGH is the opposite of smooth and of soft. **Rough** means having ridges or not smooth. A **rough** road has ridges or bumps on it. It is not smooth. Hand cream makes **rough** hands soft. **Rough** also describes something that is not gentle. Football is a **rough** game.

rough

uneven
bumpy
rocky
harsh
rugged
ragged
bristly
scraggly
scaly
coarse

Uneven and **bumpy** mean not level but having some points higher than other points. *The plowed field was **uneven** and hard to walk across. We had a **bumpy** ride in a wagon.*

Rocky means full of rocks or stones. *The water splashed on the **rocky** beach.*

Harsh is rough and without smoothness or gentleness. *He spoke in a **harsh** voice when he was angry. The two boys said **harsh** words to each other. Going without supper is **harsh** punishment.*

Rugged means having a rough, uneven surface. *In the mountains there is much **rugged** country.*
Rugged can also mean hard or harsh. *The Pilgrims suffered through the rough, **rugged** winter.* Perhaps this is where the term "rough it" came from. Today we "rough it" when we mean camp out in a tent or live without the comforts of home.

scraggly

Ragged can also mean having rough or uneven edges. *The nail tore a **ragged** hole in my coat.*

Bristly is rough with short, coarse hair. *My dog feels **bristly**. Dad's face feels **bristly** if he doesn't shave.*

Scraggly means uncared for. *The girl's **scraggly** hair looked as if it had never been brushed.*

Scaly is rough with scales. A fish feels **scaly** when you touch it.

Coarse means rough to the touch or made up of large pieces. It is the opposite of fine. You would call a piece of cloth **coarse** if it felt rough or scratchy. One that felt smooth is fine. A beach that has **coarse** sand is not as pleasant to walk on as one with fine sand. **Coarse** is the opposite of delicate or dainty when it means roughly made or done. **Coarse,** heavy thread would not be used to make delicate lace. An artist can draw a face with a few **coarse,** heavy lines of a brush or pen. But he would use a fine brush or pen to make thin, delicate lines.

coarse

fine

Look up HARD for other words you can sometimes use instead.

ANTONYMS: smooth, soft, delicate, dainty, gentle, fine

173

RUCKUS	Look up NOISE.
RUGGED	Look up ROUGH.
RUN	RUN means go faster than walk. You **run** to catch the bus if you are late. Ball players **run** to base or **run** to catch the ball. You probably **ran** somewhere yesterday. Perhaps you **have run** all the way to school on many mornings when you have overslept.

Run can also mean move or work. Water **runs** from a faucet. A motor **runs.**

jog
sprint
race
trot
lope
gallop
bolt
flee
chase
operate
work
go

Jog means run slowly. If you were running just for fun on a nice day, you might *jog* down the street. Athletes often *jog* along the road for exercise.

Sprint means run at top speed for a short distance. In a long race, a runner might *jog* along at first and then suddenly *sprint* to the finish line.

Race means move or run at the highest speed possible, usually to beat someone. If two boys *race* to the corner, each one is trying to run faster than the other and to get there first. If your mother needs flour to bake a cake, you may *race* to the store for some. When the phone rings, some people *race* to answer it.

race

A horse *trots* when he moves along between a walk and a run. He *lopes* if he moves with an easy, steady stride. He *gallops* if he runs at top speed. People use these words to describe the way human beings run, too. A small child walking with his father may *trot* to keep up with him. A man may *lope* down the street to catch a bus. Children *gallop* when they pretend they are riding horses.

Bolt, flee, and *chase* can also mean run. *Bolt* means move away suddenly. *The frightened horse bolted, and his owner had to chase him. Flee* means run away. People *flee* from a burning house. *Chase* means run fast after something. Dogs *chase* cats. Men often have to *chase* their hats on a windy day.

Operate and *work* sometimes may be used instead of run or make something run. Many radios *operate* or *work* on batteries. A wristwatch won't *work* or run if you forget to wind it. Men in factories *operate* machines when they run them.

operate

Go can also mean run if you say your watch is going.

ANTONYMS: stop, remain, stay

RUSH   Look up HURRY.

175

SAD

unhappy
downcast
melancholy
mournful
sorrowful
sorry
miserable
wretched
forlorn
woebegone

SAD is the opposite of <u>happy</u>. There are many other words you might use to describe how you feel when you're **unhappy** or sad about something.

Downcast really means "thrown down." When you are **downcast,** you do feel as if something were pushing you or throwing you down.

Melancholy means sad and thoughtful. Thinking about how lonely you'll be without your best friend may put you in a **melancholy** mood.

Mournful and **sorrowful** mean full of sadness and mourning for something. *The boy played a **mournful** tune on his guitar. You could tell by the girl's **sorrowful** expression that she was not going to the party.*

Sorry can mean feeling sad because of something you have said or done, and wishing you had not said or done it. *The girl was **sorry** she broke her sister's watch.* When you hurt someone's feelings and say you're sorry, you probably feel unhappy and sad. But if you accidentally step on someone's toe, or bump into someone, it is polite to say you are sorry. This

miserable

doesn't mean you're really sad, but it's a considerate way of excusing yourself.

If you are *miserable* or *wretched,* you are full of misery or are extremely unhappy about something or with something. A cold can make you feel *miserable.* You might feel *miserable* because you said something unkind to a friend. *It was a* *miserable* *night for walking. I feel* *wretched* *because I forgot to give her an important message. We had a* *wretched* *trip in the rain.*

Forlorn means sad or lost and lonely. *There was one* *forlorn* *passenger on the bus. The* *forlorn* *look on the lost child's face almost brought tears to my eyes.*

Woebegone means very sorrowful. *Bloodhounds always look* *woebegone.*

ANTONYMS: happy, contented, cheerful, glad, merry, funny, delighted

SAFE	Look up antonyms of DANGEROUS.
SAID	SAID is the past tense and past participle of SAY.
SAIL	Look up FLY.
SANK	SANK is the past tense of SINK.
SATINY	Look up SMOOTH.
SATISFIED	Look up HAPPY.
SAUNTER	Look up WALK.
SAVE	Look up KEEP.
SAW	Look up CUT.
SAW	SAW is the past tense of SEE.

save

SAY

SAY is used so often that it has become one of the most tired words in our language. *Say* means put into words. You may say the same thing you *said* yesterday or say the same thing you *have said* every day for a week. *Say* as well as many of its synonyms can be used in two ways—with or without quotation marks. *He **said** he was ready*—this is called an indirect quotation—or *He **said**, "I am ready"*— this is called a direct quotation. *Say* is a very good word and it should be used, but writers of stories try especially hard to find some other words to use when they write conversation between characters. There are really hundreds of words that can take the place of *say* when you are writing a direct quotation.

state
declare
exclaim
remark
observe
comment
agree
suggest
begin
continue
add
shout
call
scream
shriek
yell
roar
howl

State, declare, and *exclaim* are good synonyms for *say*. You *state* a fact or you *state* your opinion just by saying in words what you know to be true or what you think is true about something. *The policeman **stated** that we were speeding. The judge **stated** the facts of the case. "This is not true," she **stated**.* You *declare* something if you say it firmly. *He **declared** he had never seen anything so funny. "I won't go another step," she **declared**.* You *exclaim* if you say something loudly or sharply. *"These are all for you," she **exclaimed** impatiently, dropping a handful of letters in my lap. When I burst into the room, Grandma **exclaimed** that I had frightened her half to death.*

Remark, observe, comment, and *agree* may often be used for say. They can all be used in either direct or indirect quotations. They all mean express an opinion in words. *"Well, this has been a wonderful day," she **remarked**. The man **remarked** that the bus*

comment

was later than usual. After Father watched us splashing in the pool for quite a while, he **observed** *that it looked very inviting but that the water seemed too shallow for diving.* "It's not quite four o'clock," *she* **observed.** "The sun is still high." "He's a good ballplayer," **commented** *Joe. Dad* **commented** *that my new dress was pretty. The television announcer* **commented** *on the news. We* **agreed** *that Jim's plan was the best, even though we didn't like it.* "All right," *she* **agreed** *with a sigh.* "You may go to the movie if you will help with the dishes first."

Suggest can mean say but it also adds the meaning of offering an idea. *I* **suggested** *that they all come along for a ride. Can you* **suggest** *a good place to eat?* "We might take a picnic lunch to the park," **suggested** *Mother.* "Who **suggested** *that we wouldn't need our raincoats?*" *asked Bob, standing in the rain.*

Begin, continue, add, are good words to use for say, even though they are not real synonyms. "Once upon a time," *the storyteller* **began.** "After Hansel and Gretel escaped from the witch," **continued** *the storyteller,* "they went on through the woods." "And they lived happily ever after!" **added** *one child, who had heard the story many times before.*

Shout and **call** mean say loudly. "Stop!" *he* **shouted.** "Breakfast is ready!" *Mother* **called.**

Scream, shriek, yell, roar, and **howl,** all may be used to say something loudly or excitedly.

Look up TALK for other words to use.

call

SCALY   Look up ROUGH.

SCANTY   Look up LITTLE.

SCARE

SCARE means cause sudden fear. It is sometimes hard to calm someone who **has been scared.** *Did the loud noise* **scare** *you? Dad* **scared** *me when he jumped up and yelled "Boo!"*

alarm
frighten
terrify

Alarm means warn of approaching danger. Sometimes it means upset someone with the thought of danger. *The firebell will* **alarm** *the townspeople. I don't wish to* **alarm** *you, but there may be some danger of a flood if this rain continues another day. She* **was alarmed** *by the smell of smoke.*

Frighten means alarm or scare. *The clap of thunder* **frightened** *the little children. We put up a scarecrow to* **frighten** *away the crows.*

Terrify means fill with terror. *The huge bear* **terrified** *the girls when it came toward them out of the woods. We* **were** *so* **terrified** *by the weird noise that we couldn't move.*

ANTONYMS: calm (v), soothe

SCARED

Look up AFRAID.

SCARY

If something frightened you, you'd probably say it was **scary.** **Scary** is a perfectly good word, but there are others you can use, too.

frightening
spooky
terrifying
horrifying

Frightening means scary. *He wore a Halloween mask that was really* **frightening.**

Spooky means scary because it makes you feel that ghosts may appear any moment. *We saw a* **spooky** *movie. It was* **spooky** *in the woods after dark.*

Terrifying and **horrifying** are stronger than scary. A **terrifying** noise fills you with terror. A **horrifying** sight fills you with horror.

SCRAGGLY	Look up ROUGH.
SCREAM	Look up SAY and SHOUT.
SEE	Look up LOOK.
SEEN	SEEN is the past participle of SEE.
SEIZE	Look up CATCH.
SELECT	Look up CHOOSE.

seize

SEND

SEND means make something or someone move from where you are to some other place. A mother **sends** her child to school. *Indians **sent** arrows zipping across the plains. Scientists **have sent** rockets out into space.* You might **send** flowers to a sick friend.

mail
ship
transmit
dispatch

Mail means send a package or letter to the post office so that it may be delivered to the person you are sending it to.

Ship means put something aboard a ship or plane or some other vehicle to send it from one place to another. You'd **ship** a trunk or **mail** a package, but you'd never **mail** or **ship** an arrow through the air.

Transmit means send from one place or from one person to another. It also means send out signals. *If you will **transmit** the message to me, I will send it on.* Sailors **transmit** storm warnings by radio.

dispatch

Dispatch means send off or away. *The king **dispatched** his messenger with a note for the queen.* Some people **dispatch** messages by sending a carrier pigeon that will fly straight to its home loft with a message tied to its leg.

Look up CARRY for other words you might use.

ANTONYMS: receive, get

181

SENT	SENT is the past tense and past participle of SEND.
SET	Look up PUT. SET is the same in the past tense and in the past-participle form.

set out

SET UP	Look up MAKE.
SEVERE	Look up HARD and BAD and AWFUL.
SHADOWY	Look up DIM.
SHADY	Look up DIM. Look up antonyms of BRIGHT.
SHAPE	Look up MAKE.
SHATTER	Look up BREAK.
SHINY	Look up BRIGHT. Look up antonyms of DIM.
SHIP	Look up SEND.
SHOOT	Look up THROW.
SHOT	SHOT is the past tense and past participle of SHOOT.

shoot

182

SHOUT

SHOUT means cry out loudly. It's the opposite of whisper. You might **shout** at a friend across the street. People often **shout** at each other if they lose their tempers. You have to **shout** when you talk to a person who can't hear well. When you cry out or shout, you most likely say words or sentences that can be understood. You might **shout** "Hurray!" if you were happy, or "What?" if you were surprised, or "Get out!" if you were angry.

call
scream
shriek
yell
yodel

Call means make a sound with your voice in order to get someone's attention—***call*** for help or ***call*** your dog. *"Wait a minute," Mother **called** from the doorway. "Hurry back!" he **called** as we drove away. She **called** to me from her window.*

If you ***scream*** or ***shriek*** or ***yell,*** you call out at the top of your lungs. You could say actual words or you could just make a long, loud sound. *She **screamed** with delight when she saw the birthday cake. We **shrieked** when we started downhill on the roller coaster. The policeman **yelled** at us when we ran into the street.*

Yodel is a special way to shout. It is done by shifting your voice to a very high note then back to your regular pitch. By constantly shifting back and forth you make a kind of wavy sound. People living in the mountains often ***yodel,*** and the sound echoes from peak to peak.

Look up SAY to see if some other words would fit better what you mean.

ANTONYM: whisper

shriek

SHOVE

Look up PUSH.

183

SHOW

SHOW means be seen or let something be seen. Happiness or sadness may *show* on a person's face. Or a person may *show* his anger even though he tries to conceal or hide it. A baby's actions may *show* that he is sleepy.

point out
demonstrate
present
display
exhibit
direct
lead
guide
reveal
prove

Point out means show something that has not been seen or understood before. In a strange city someone might *point out* the most interesting sights.

Demonstrate means show how something is done. A scout leader builds a fire to *demonstrate* how it is done. A football coach might use movies to *point out* what players were doing wrong. He would *demonstrate* how to kick a football.

Present and *display* can be used when someone is showing objects to people. Stores *present* the latest fashions for people to look at. A theater *presents* a movie. A storekeeper *displays* things he wants to sell so customers will know what he has. He often *displays* objects in his windows.

Exhibit means show something publicly. Artists *exhibit* their work.

exhibit

184

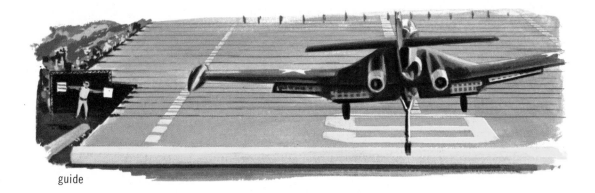

guide

Direct, lead, and *guide* mean show or help someone find the way to wherever he is going. A policeman *directs* traffic. He would *direct* you to a place you want to go, but he would not go with you. If you *lead* someone, you usually go ahead of him. You *lead* a horse by holding it with a strap to make sure it follows you. You *guide* someone when you know all the places where he might have trouble or get lost and you help him get past them safely. A man *guides* a plane when it lands on a carrier deck. A fireman may *lead* people out of a burning building. He would *guide* them down a ladder.

Reveal means bring to light or make known something that has been concealed or should be hidden. A flashlight's beam *reveals* the inside of a cave. Some people *reveal* secrets.

Prove means show by finding and pointing out facts. When you disagree with someone about something and can find some facts that show you are right, you can *prove* your point. If you brag about being able to run faster than anyone in your class, you may have to *prove* it by doing so.

ANTONYMS: hide, mask, conceal

185

SHOWY	Look up LOUD.
SHRIEK	Look up SAY and SHOUT.
SHRILL	Look up LOUD.
SHUFFLE	Look up WALK.
SHUT	SHUT means move into place so there is no opening or so nothing can go through or past. You **shut** a window to keep cold air out. Perhaps you also **shut** it yesterday. You **have shut** it twice today. A person **shuts** his eyes to keep out the light. You **shut off** the water when you turn a faucet. You pull down a curtain to **shut out** the sunshine. *A pile of rocks* **shut off** *our only path to freedom. By the time he* **had shut** *the door, the floor was covered with snow.*

shut

close *slam* *bar* *block* *imprison*	*Close* means shut off an opening or passage or end something. *The city may* **close** *the road for repairs.* You **close** something by bringing two ends or sides together. ***Close*** *your fist.* ***Close*** *the book. She pulled a zipper to* **close** *her jacket. The circus* **closes** *today.* A door **slams** if the wind pushes it shut very hard and fast. An angry person may **slam** a drawer shut or **slam** down the cover of a box.

186

Bar means shut out. A bar is put across an opening to stop something from going in or out. *Pioneers barred the doors of their cabins.*
Cowboys *bar* the gate to keep horses in a corral.

Block means shut off or hinder someone from going forward. *A big truck blocked the road.*
The giant standing in the doorway blocked our way.

block

Imprison means shut in so no escape is possible.
An explosion imprisoned five men in the mine.
Look up STOP for other words you might use.
ANTONYMS: open, unfasten

SHY	Look up QUIET (adj).
SILENT	Look up QUIET (adj). Look up antonyms of LOUD.
SILKY	Look up SMOOTH.
SILLY	Look up STUPID.
SIMPLE	Look up antonyms of HARD.
SINK	Look up FALL.
SIZZLING	Look up HOT.
SKILLED	Look up GOOD.

SKIM	Look up FLY.
SKIMPY	Look up LITTLE.
SKINNY	Look up THIN.
SKIP	Look up JUMP.
SLAM	Look up SHUT.
SLASH	Look up CUT.
SLEEK	Look up SMOOTH.
SLENDER	Look up THIN.
SLICE	Look up CUT.
SLICK	Look up SMOOTH.
SLIM	Look up THIN.
SLIPPERY	Look up SMOOTH.

slash

SLIT	Look up CUT. SLIT is the same in the past tense and in the past-participle form.
SLOPPY	Look up CARELESS and WET.
SLOW (adj)	Look up antonyms of FAST (adj).
SLOW (adv)	Look up antonyms of FAST (adv).
SLOW DOWN	Look up antonyms of HURRY.
SLOWLY	Look up antonyms of FAST (adv).
SLUGGISH	Look up antonyms of FAST (adj).
SLUGGISHLY	Look up antonyms of FAST (adv).
SMALL	Look up LITTLE. Look up antonyms of LARGE and of GREAT.
SMART (adj)	SMART means able to learn easily and to understand and solve problems. It is the

opposite of stupid. *The **smart** pup found his master, who was hiding behind the garage. Roy is a **smart** boy. His science project was good.*

intelligent
bright
brilliant
wise
clever
quick-witted

Intelligent means smart and able to think clearly, understand, and make good decisions. If a person is not very **intelligent** or smart, he may be called dumb. But even a smart person can easily make a dumb mistake.

Bright is often used to mean smart. Then it is the opposite of dull. *It was a **bright** idea to build a Clubhouse. A **bright** pupil has no excuse for getting bad marks in school.*

Brilliant is stronger than bright. Something or someone very outstanding is called **brilliant**. *She made some **brilliant** remarks at dinner. He is a **brilliant** musician.*

brilliant

Wise means able to understand people and able to understand things that happen. A **wise** person usually knows how to deal with them.

Clever means quick to think of something or skillful at doing something. *The **clever** boy had an idea for a Columbus Day program. She is **clever** at making clothes.*

Quick-witted means quick to think and understand. A **quick-witted** person may guess a riddle fast.

ANTONYMS: stupid, dull, dumb, dim-witted

SMART (v)	Look up HURT.
SMASH	Look up BREAK.
SMEARED	Look up DIRTY.
SMILE	Look up LAUGH.
SMOKY	Look up DIM.

smeared

SMOOTH

level
flat
even
polished
slippery
slick
sleek
creamy
silky
satiny
velvety

SMOOTH is the opposite of rough. **Smooth** means having a surface without high and low points. The sea is **smooth** when there are no waves. Waves make a rough sea.

Level and **flat** mean having no parts higher or lower than the rest. *The recipe called for a **level** teaspoonful of sugar. Airplanes need **level** ground to land on. A baseball diamond is **flat.***

Something is **even** if it is regular or uniform and smooth. An **even** sidewalk is easy to skate on. Someone with an **even** temper does not get angry very often.

Polished means smooth and shiny. **Polished** furniture is smooth to the touch.

Slippery describes something so smooth it is hard to hold on to. Ice is **slippery** to walk on. An object covered with oil or grease is so smooth it is **slippery** to hold on to.

Slick can mean slippery, too. When you talk about someone looking **slick** or **sleek,** though, you usually mean looking neat and well dressed. A dog or cat or horse has a **sleek** coat if its hair is smooth and shiny.

Creamy means like cream, which is smooth. Fudge is **creamy** candy. It feels **creamy** in your mouth.

Silky, satiny, velvety, all describe some surface that feels or looks as smooth as silk or satin or velvet. Anything **silky** or **satiny** probably is shiny. Something **velvety** is smooth and soft. Hair is often called **silky.** A leaf might be **satiny.** A rose petal is **velvety.**

Look up SOFT for other words to use.

ANTONYMS: rough, bumpy, harsh, uneven, wrinkled

slippery

SMUDGED	Look up DIRTY.
SNATCH	Look up CATCH.
SNICKER	Look up LAUGH.
SNIP	Look up CUT.
SOAKING	Look up WET.
SOAR	Look up FLY.

soaking

SOFT

SOFT means not hard or rough or severe or loud. A baby's skin is *soft.* Pudding is *soft.* Silk, satin, and velvet are *soft* to touch. Some cloth is coarse and rough. On a summer evening the air feels *soft.* An icy wind can make air feel harsh. A person with a *soft* voice does not speak roughly or too loud. It is easy to walk on firm ground, but hard to walk in *soft* mud.

fleecy
fluffy
mild
gentle
lenient

We call big, white, soft-looking clouds *fleecy.* A *fleecy* blanket feels good on a cold night. Mashed potatoes should be *fluffy. I like a fluffy pillow on my bed.*

Mild and *gentle* mean not hard or rough. A *mild* climate does not ever get too hot or too cold. A *mild* man does not often get angry. *He gave his horse a gentle tap with his whip.* A nurse putting a bandage on someone's cut finger would be *gentle* when she touched the sore spot.

Lenient means not harsh or severe. *His parents were too lenient when they let him do whatever he wanted. They should have been more firm.*

Look up SMOOTH for other words that might be better for what you want to say.

ANTONYMS: hard, rough, coarse, loud, firm, harsh, stern

fluffy

191

SOGGY	Look up WET.
SOILED	Look up DIRTY. Look up antonyms of CLEAN.
SOLID	Look up HARD.
SOLUTION	Look up ANSWER (n).
SOLVE	Look up ANSWER (v).
SOOTHE	Look up antonyms of SCARE.
SORROWFUL	Look up SAD. Look up antonyms of HAPPY.
SORRY	Look up SAD.
SOUNDLESS	Look up QUIET (adj).
SPARKLING	Look up BRIGHT.
SPEAK	Look up TALK.
SPECTACULAR	Look up WONDERFUL.
SPED	SPED is the past tense and past participle of SPEED.
SPEECHLESS	Look up QUIET (adj).
SPEED	Look up HURRY.
SPEEDILY	Look up FAST (adv).
SPEEDY	Look up FAST (adj).
SPICK-AND-SPAN	Look up CLEAN. Look up antonyms of DIRTY.
SPLENDID	Look up WONDERFUL.
SPOIL	Look up HURT.

soggy

SPOILED	Look up BAD.
SPOKE	SPOKE is the past tense of SPEAK.
SPOKEN	SPOKEN is the past participle of SPEAK.
SPOOKY	Look up SCARY.

spooky

SPOTLESS	Look up CLEAN.
SPOTTED	Look up DIRTY.
SPRANG	SPRANG is the past tense of SPRING.
SPREAD	Look up PUT. SPREAD is the same in the past tense and in the past-participle form.
SPRING	Look up START and JUMP.
SPRINT	Look up RUN.
SPRUNG	SPRUNG is the past participle of SPRING.

SQUABBLE	Look up FIGHT.
STAGGER	Look up WALK.
STAINED	Look up DIRTY.
STALK	Look up WALK.
STARE	Look up LOOK.

stagger

START

START means make the first movement from a still position. You *start* down the stairs when you go down the first step. You *start* on a trip when you leave home. Runners in a race *start* when the gun goes off. A gun *starts* the race.

Start also means do something for the first time. *We started going to the swimming pool last year.*

Start can mean come or bring into being. A river *starts* from a tiny stream. A group of men often can *start* a newspaper.

Other words are better to use than *start* for some of these meanings.

begin
open
rise
spring
originate
introduce
invent
create
turn on
launch
establish

Begin means start something that may go on for some time. If you *begin* something you usually finish it. But something that *begins* usually ends. For example you *begin* a book. When you have read it all, you have finished it. But the book *begins* on page 1 and ends on page 200.

The story of America begins with Columbus. Jim began to write a letter. School begins in September. It has begun to rain again.

Open can mean start or begin something. A person can *open* a new store. If business is bad, he may close it soon. A new play *opens* at a theater. A show can *open* with a magician's act or with acrobats. It may conclude or end with a grand finale.

Rise, spring, and *originate* mean start or come into being. Some rivers *rise* from mountain streams. Plants *spring* from seeds. Many modern ideas *originated* in the past.

You *introduce* something when you bring it to the attention of people who did not know or think about

introduce

it before. *The girls **introduced** a new fashion when they wore socks of different colors.* You **introduce** two people who do not know each other.

Invent and ***create*** mean bring something into being. A man usually ***invents*** a machine to make some work easier. A man may ***create*** something just for the sake of beauty. The sewing machine ***was invented.*** A beautiful statue or painting ***is created*** by a sculptor or artist.

You ***turn on*** a motor to start it running.

To ***launch*** a boat you put it into the water for the first time. You can also ***launch*** a program or a project when you start it.

Establish means start some new idea or custom or thing. People ***establish*** schools and churches. Pilgrims ***established*** colonies in the New World.

Look up MAKE for other words to use.

ANTONYMS: stop, end (v), finish, close, conclude

STATE	Look up SAY.
STATELY	Look up GREAT.
STAY	Look up antonyms of RUN and of GO.
STEAMING	Look up HOT.
STEP	Look up WALK.
STERN	Look up HARD. Look up antonyms of SOFT.
STIFF	Look up HARD.
STILL	Look up QUIET (adj). Look up antonyms of LOUD.

step

STILLNESS	Look up antonyms of NOISE.
STING	Look up HURT.
STOP	STOP means not go on or not let something go on. You *stop* talking when class begins. Cars *stop* when a traffic light is red. An umpire may have to *stop* a fight. You *stop* a leak in the roof or in a tire.

end
conclude
cease
pause
discontinue
quit
halt
prevent
arrest

If something **ends,** it stops and does not start again. *The story begins and* **ends** *on the desert.* You **end** or **conclude** something by stopping it. *We* **ended** *our conversation quickly. The author* **concluded** *his book on a happy note.* **Conclude** usually means finish something, but **end** can mean stop something whether it is finished or not.

Cease can mean stop or come to an end gradually. *The ticking of our clock got slower and slower; then it* **ceased.** *The roar of the crowd died down and finally* **ceased.**

You **pause** if you stop doing something for a minute or two and then continue. *As we passed the store, we* **paused** *to look in the windows. He* **paused** *to take a drink of water, then went on speaking.*

pause

196

discontinue

If you stop something you have been doing regularly, you *discontinue* it. *The school cafeteria* **discontinued** *serving lunch. We forgot to* **discontinue** *the newspaper and milk deliveries when we went away.*

Quit means stop or give up something. You can *quit* a job or *quit* taking music lessons. *They* **quit** *talking when the principal came in.* **Has** *your brother* **quit** *teasing you?*

Halt usually means stop or bring to a sudden stop. *The soldiers marched across the field and then* **halted.** *The policeman told the fleeing robber to* **halt.**

Prevent means stop something from moving or happening. *Ropes* **prevented** *the crowd from getting too close to the fire.*

Arrest means stop or capture. It also means bring to a stop or slow down. *The sheriff* **arrested** *a cowboy and took him to jail.* A cloud of smoke coming from a building may *arrest* your attention as you pass by. *Doctors tried to* **arrest** *the infection.*

You may find better words for what you want to say if you look up END (v) and SHUT.

ANTONYMS: go, start, begin, continue

197

STOUT	Look up STRONG. Look up antonyms of THIN.
STRAIN	Look up PULL.
STRANGE	Look up QUEER.
STRAY	Look up GO.
STRETCH	Look up PULL.
STRIDDEN	STRIDDEN is the past participle of STRIDE.
STRIDE	Look up WALK.
STRODE	STRODE is the past tense of STRIDE.
STROLL	Look up WALK.
STRONG	STRONG means having great power or strength. *Grandmother likes to drink* **strong** *tea, but I like* <u>*weak*</u> *tea.* *The piano movers have to be very* **strong** *men.* *A* <u>*frail*</u> *man could not lift much.*

strong   frail

stout *sturdy* *tough* *forceful* *powerful* *hardy*	**Stout** sometimes means brave and strong. *The sailors had* **stout** *hearts. They would not give up.* It also means firm. A **stout** stick helps you walk over rough ground. You need a **stout** ladder. **Sturdy** means strong and firm. *That* **sturdy** *tree has lived for many years.* A **sturdy** box is well made. One that is not well made is <u>flimsy</u>.

198

Tough means firm and strong and able to resist anything that tries to break it. *Shoes made of **tough** leather will wear well.* A **tough** boxer is one who does not give up or lose easily. **Tough** meat is very hard to chew.

Forceful means full of strength or force. *The speaker had a **forceful** manner. His voice was not weak or feeble. A **forceful** wind tore at the shutters.*

Powerful means full of strength and power. *The tractor was so **powerful** it leveled the sand piles in fifteen minutes. A mad elephant is **powerful** enough to pull a tree out of the ground.*

powerful

Hardy means strong and healthy, able to stand up against difficult things. *The girl is **hardy** now, but she was very frail when she was a baby.* A **hardy** plant can live through very cold weather.

ANTONYMS: weak, feeble, frail, flimsy

STUFFED	Look up FULL.
STUMBLE	Look up WALK.
STUNG	STUNG is the past tense and past participle of STING.

STUPID | STUPID means very slow to understand and learn. *He felt **stupid** because he couldn't do the math problem.* Something without sense can also be called **stupid.** *Instead of saying something **stupid,** she came up with a* brilliant *idea. It seemed as if the **stupid** play would never end.*

dull
dim-witted
dumb
silly
foolish
crazy

Dull can mean slow in thinking or learning or acting. *Some people are **dull** when they first wake up.* When something is not interesting, it is **dull** and uninteresting. *Many books are **dull.***

Dim-witted means not thinking clearly. *That **dim-witted** cat should be chasing mice instead of dogs.*

dim-witted

Dumb is often used in place of stupid, especially to describe someone who can't say what he means. *Her sudden appearance left me **dumb**—with nothing to say. My answer to your surprising question must have sounded pretty **dumb.***

Silly, foolish, and ***crazy*** mean without sense or thought. *What a **silly** thing to say! That **silly** girl giggles all the time. Going without a coat was **foolish.** She made a **foolish** mistake. Riding your bike on the wrong side of the road is a **crazy** thing to do.*

ANTONYMS: smart (adj), bright, clever, brilliant

200

STURDY	Look up STRONG.
SUBDUED	Look up QUIET (adj). Look up antonyms of LOUD.
SUDDEN	Look up FAST (adj).
SUDDENLY	Look up FAST (adv).
SUGGEST	Look up SAY.
SULTRY	Look up HOT.
SUNK	SUNK is the past participle of SINK.
SUNNY	Look up BRIGHT.
SUPERB	Look up WONDERFUL.
SUPPORT	Look up HELP.
SUPPOSE	Look up THINK.
SWELTERING	Look up HOT. Look up antonyms of COLD.
SWIFT	Look up FAST (adj).
SWIFTLY	Look up FAST (adv).
SWINDLE	Look up GYP.
SYMPATHETIC	Look up KIND.

sympathetic

TACTFUL	Look up KIND.
TAKE	Look up CARRY.
TAKE APART	Look up antonyms of MAKE.
TAKE AWAY	Look up antonyms of PUT.
TAKEN	TAKEN is the past participle of TAKE.
TAKE OFF	Look up GO.

TALK

talk

TALK means express a thought or share ideas with someone by using your voice and forming words. *Talk* usually suggests that you say words to someone who listens to you and then replies. People *talk* to each other. But it is possible to *talk* to someone or to something that does not listen or reply. You can *talk* to your dog or *talk* to yourself or *talk* to a baby. Little girls often *talk* to their dolls. You can also *talk* to a group. *A fireman **talked** to our class about fire prevention.* You *talk to* someone or something. You *talk about* something—*about* homework or *about* vacation.

202

speak
tell
chat
gossip
comment
discuss
argue
dispute
quarrel

chat

Speak means say words whether you are talking to someone or not. You can *speak* fast or *speak* louder. Some people *speak* several languages. You *speak* to a friend if you say "Hi" when you meet him on the street. Maybe you both stop and talk, or maybe you go right on.

Tell usually means give information to someone by speaking. You could *tell* your brother a bedtime story or *tell* the class about something you saw on the street.

Chat and *gossip* mean talk about something interesting but usually not very important. Perhaps you *chat* with a friend every evening over the telephone until someone tells you to hang up. You *gossip* if you talk about somebody or tell secrets that friends have trusted you not to tell.

Comment means speak your opinion or tell what you think about something. You might *comment* on a friend's new shoes or on a book you have read or on how nice someone looks.

Discuss means talk about some subject and think about all sides of a question. *The committee discussed plans for our spring project. We discussed the problem of finding a playground.*

Argue, dispute, and *quarrel* are stronger than discuss. You *argue* with someone when you tell him all the reasons why you are right and he is wrong. When he tells you what he thinks is right, you *dispute* everything he says, and probably you both get angry enough to *quarrel.* Everyone knows you *are quarreling* when you shout at each other.

Look up SAY for other words you might use.

TAME	Look up QUIET (adj).
TEAR	Look up BREAK.
TEAR DOWN	Look up antonyms of MAKE.
TELL	Look up TALK.
TEND	Look up KEEP.
TENDER	Look up antonyms of HARD.
TEPID	Look up HOT.
TERRIBLE	Look up AWFUL.
TERRIFIED	Look up AFRAID.
TERRIFY	Look up SCARE.
TERRIFYING	Look up SCARY.
THICK	Look up antonyms of THIN.

tame

THIN   THIN describes something that has just a little distance through it or from one side of it to the other. You would spray a *thin* stream of water on a garden that you had just planted. A heavy stream would wash out the seeds.

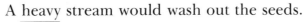

thin

You can draw a **thin** line or a heavy, thick line. **Thin** paper is easy to see through.

lean
skinny
slender
slim
fine
narrow

Lean and **skinny** mean not fat. **Lean** meat does not have much fat. A very thin person is sometimes called **lean** but is usually called **skinny.** Probably no one would ask for a piece of **skinny** meat.

Slender and **slim** describe something narrower in width than in length or height. **Slim** can also mean small or not important. *We have a slim chance of winning the game.* A **slim** package is easier to carry than a bulky one.

slim

bulky

Fine means thin or slender. **Fine** thread might be no thicker than a hair, but coarse thread is almost as thick as string. A baby's hairbrush has **fine** bristles. **Fine** wire is good for hanging small pictures. But you would need heavy or stout wire for hanging big pictures.

Narrow means not very wide or far across. A **narrow** street does not have much room for cars to pass each other.

ANTONYMS: fat, thick, heavy, wide, broad, plump, stout, bushy, bulky

THINK

THINK is a word everyone knows. Probably
everyone has times, though, when he doesn't do it.
Think means use your mind to form a thought or
idea. It means decide what to do or decide how you
feel about something. Perhaps you *thought* about
something yesterday or *have thought* about it often.
Here are some good words to use for different ways
to think.

believe
suppose
imagine
wonder
guess
consider
ponder
plan

Believe, suppose, and *imagine* mean think that
something is probably true. You may not be able to
prove it, but from whatever facts you do have, you
form an opinion about it. *Believe* is the strongest
word. If a person *believes* in someone or in some
idea, he has firm faith that whatever he thinks is
true. If you *suppose* or *imagine* something is true, you
think it probably is because it seems to be and no
one has proved that it isn't. You may *suppose* a story
is true because you read it in the newspaper. You
imagine that it will rain if black clouds cover the sky.

Wonder is think about something when you
don't know for sure what is true. You *wonder*
what you will be when you grow up. You *wonder*
what it feels like to be a butterfly. You *wonder* if
you wrote the wrong answer on a test.

Guess is make up your mind about something
without any facts to base your opinion on. You
guess it won't rain on your birthday. You might
guess how fast a car is going as it passes the
house, or *guess* how far it is from here to the
farthest star.

Consider and *ponder* mean think about something
very seriously and very hard. If you had something

206

tremendously important to do or decide, you would *consider* it carefully and for quite a while.

You might *ponder* it for several days and *consider* every side of it before making up your mind.

Plan means think about something you are going to do and arrange all the steps or parts in order. Someone who *plans* a vacation thinks about where to go, how to get there, what to take along, and many other things.

plan

THOUGHT	THOUGHT is the past tense and past participle of THINK.
THOUGHTFUL	Look up KIND. Look up antonyms of CARELESS.
THOUGHTLESS	Look up CARELESS.
THREW	THREW is the past tense of THROW.
THRILLING	Look up INTERESTING.

THROW

THROW means make something go through the air by movement of the arm and hand. *Let's **throw** darts at a target. You **threw** your cap on the table, didn't you? The children **have thrown** their coats on a chair.* There are different ways to **throw.**

fling
hurl
pitch
toss
shoot
pass

Fling and **hurl** mean throw hard and without caring just where the object goes. If you make a mistake while writing a letter, you may crumple the paper and **fling** it at the wastebasket. You would **hurl** something that is heavy. *The giant picked up a rock and **hurled** it down the mountainside.*

hurl

You **pitch** something when you aim carefully and try to hit a certain spot. You might **pitch** stones at a tree.

Toss means throw very lightly or easily. You would **toss** a beachball to a very small child or **toss** an eraser to a person sitting near you.

Shoot, pitch, and **pass** are used to mean throw in some games. A player **shoots** a basket when he throws the basketball through the hoop. A pitcher **pitches** when he throws the baseball for the batter to hit it. A football player **passes** when he throws the football to another member of his team.

THROW ASIDE	Look up antonyms of CHOOSE.
THROW AWAY	Look up antonyms of KEEP.
THROWN	THROWN is the past participle of THROW.
THRUST	Look up PUSH. THRUST is the same in the past tense and in the past-participle form.
THUNDEROUS	Look up LOUD.
TIMID	Look up AFRAID. Look up antonyms of BRAVE.
TINY	Look up LITTLE. Look up antonyms of LARGE.
TIP	Look up END (n).
TIPTOE	Look up WALK.
TOLD	TOLD is the past tense and past participle of TELL.
TOOK	TOOK is the past tense of TAKE.
TOPPLE	Look up FALL.
TORE	TORE is the past tense of TEAR.
TORN	TORN is the past participle of TEAR.
TORRID	Look up HOT. Look up antonyms of COLD.
TOSS	Look up THROW.
TOTE	Look up CARRY.
TOUGH	Look up STRONG and HARD.
TOUR	Look up TRIP.

tiptoe

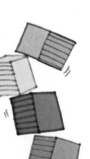

topple

TOW	Look up PULL.
TRANSMIT	Look up SEND.
TRANSPORT	Look up CARRY.
TRAP	Look up CATCH.
TRAVEL (n)	Look up TRIP.
TRAVEL (v)	Look up GO.
TREMENDOUS	Look up GREAT.
TRICK	Look up GYP.

tow

TRIP

A *trip* is the act of going from where you are to somewhere else. There are many kinds of *trips* and many words to use.

travel
journey
tour
voyage
cruise
flight
expedition
excursion
jaunt
outing
ramble

Travel is a word that means any kind of going from place to place. You may speak of air *travel.* You may read about the *travels* of someone. *Travel* may be a hobby for some people.

Journey means a trip from one place to another. Even the word itself has traveled a long way. It started out in the days of the Romans, when it was a word that meant "day." Then it went to France. The French word for "day" became "*jour,*" and "*journée*" meant "a day's travel." Now the word *journey* means a trip, no matter how long it is or how long it takes.

If you take a *journey,* you go from one certain place to another. If you take a *tour,* you go on a trip from place to place, stopping several times before the *tour* is finished. Some *tours* end at the place from which they started.

210

expedition

A *voyage* is usually a long trip by water. Going to Europe on an ocean liner is a *voyage.*

A *cruise* is a voyage from place to place. On a Great Lakes *cruise* you visit several cities.

A *flight* is a trip by air. On a tour you might take several *flights.*

An *expedition* is a trip for some special purpose. Explorers have gone on *expeditions* to the South Pole to learn more about the earth. Scientists go on *expeditions* to find ancient buried cities. You may go on a shopping *expedition* before school begins.

An *excursion* and a *jaunt* are short trips for having fun. Perhaps you take a *jaunt* to the beach or to the country some weekend. An *excursion* to the city or to the mountains may be a good trip for a short vacation.

An *outing* is an excursion usually with a picnic lunch in the open air. In the summer your class may plan an *outing* in the park or at someone's farm.

A *ramble* is usually a walk or moving around going nowhere in particular. *Today was perfect for a ramble in the park.*

TRIVIAL	Look up antonyms of GREAT and of IMPORTANT.
TROT	Look up RUN.
TRUDGE	Look up WALK.
TUG	Look up PULL.
TUMBLE	Look up FALL.
TURN ON	Look up START.

turn on

UGLY	Look up antonyms of BEAUTIFUL and of KIND.
UNAFRAID	Look up antonyms of AFRAID.
UNATTRACTIVE	Look up antonyms of BEAUTIFUL.
UNCLEAN	Look up antonyms of CLEAN.
UNCOVER	Look up FIND.
UNEARTH	Look up FIND.
UNEVEN	Look up ROUGH. Look up antonyms of SMOOTH.
UNFASTEN	Look up antonyms of SHUT.
UNFRIENDLY	Look up COLD.
UNHAPPY	Look up SAD. Look up antonyms of HAPPY.

unearth

UNHURRIED	Look up antonyms of FAST (adj).
UNIMPORTANT	Look up antonyms of IMPORTANT.
UNINTERESTING	Look up antonyms of INTERESTING.
UNJUST	Look up antonyms of RIGHT.
UNKIND	Look up antonyms of KIND.

212

UNLOADED	Look up antonyms of FULL.
UNMASK	Look up antonyms of HIDE.
UNPLEASANT	Look up antonyms of KIND.
UNRUFFLED	Look up antonyms of MAD.
UNSAFE	Look up DANGEROUS.
UNSPOTTED	Look up CLEAN.
UNSTAINED	Look up CLEAN.
UNTIDY	Look up antonyms of CLEAN.
UNUSUAL	Look up QUEER.
UPROAR	Look up NOISE.
USEFUL	Look up GOOD.

VACANT	Look up EMPTY. Look up antonyms of FULL.
VALUABLE	Look up GOOD and IMPORTANT.
VANISH	Look up GO.
VAST	Look up LARGE.
VAULT	Look up JUMP.
VELVETY	Look up SMOOTH.
VIEW	Look up LOOK.
VIRTUALLY	Look up ABOUT.
VIVID	Look up BRIGHT. Look up antonyms of DIM.
VOYAGE	Look up TRIP.

view

WALK

step
march
stride
tiptoe
stalk
amble
saunter
stroll
hike
clump
trudge
shuffle
lurch
stumble
stagger
limp
hobble

WALK means move along on foot. You *step* when you raise your feet, one after the other, and put them down in another place. When you take steps, you are walking. When someone tells you to "*Step* lively!" he means walk faster. When he says, "*Step* this way," he means for you to follow him.

March means walk steadily, with a regular step. Soldiers *march* when they walk to the beat of a drum. You *march* up the street if you walk without slowing down or without hurrying.

Stride means take long steps. A boy might *stride* along to keep up with his father.

Tiptoe means walk on your toes. *He tiptoed through the room where the baby was sleeping.*

Stalk means walk stiffly and perhaps angrily. *She stalked out of the room.* It can also mean walk cautiously to follow or catch something. *Hunters stalk wild animals.*

Amble, saunter, and *stroll* mean walk easily and probably slowly for fun. You might *saunter* along a path in the park. People *stroll* on a warm summer evening. A friend may invite you to **amble** over to his house if you are out walking.

If you **hike,** you take a long walk for fun or for exercise. Scouts often **hike** through the woods and then make camp.

Clump means walk noisily and clumsily. *My little sister **clumps** around the house in a pair of Mother's old shoes.*

Trudge means walk when walking is very hard. *Children used to **trudge** miles through the snow to school.* Walking through sand on the beach would make a person **trudge.**

Shuffle means walk without raising the feet. An old person sometimes **shuffles** down the street.

Lurch, stumble, stagger, limp, and **hobble,** all mean walk unsteadily. Sometimes when you can't keep your balance you **lurch** or roll to one side. *We all **lurched** as the bus turned the corner.*

lurch

Stumble means trip. *After he missed the first step, Sam **stumbled** down the next five stairs.*

Stagger means move from side to side while walking. If you ride on a merry-go-round and get dizzy, you may *stagger* when you get off and start to walk away. *Limp* means walk putting more weight on one leg than on the other. *The runner limped over to the sidelines after twisting his ankle.* *Hobble* means move with difficulty, taking short steps. Often horses were hobbled—that is, their legs were roped together—to keep them from wandering away. You can imagine how much difficulty a horse would have walking that way, so he would *hobble*. A girl in a very tight, long skirt would *hobble*.

Jaywalk is something no one really wants to do. Before automobiles were invented, everyone crossed streets without going to a corner. It was easy to stay out of the way of horses and buggies. But automobiles made streets dangerous to cross. Years ago, at the time automobiles began to appear on the streets, the slang word *jay* was used by almost everyone. It meant a stupid person. *Jaywalk* became a word for crossing streets carelessly.

WANT	Look up LIKE.
WAR	Look up FIGHT.
WARM	Look up HOT. Look up antonyms of COLD.
WATCH	Look up LOOK.
WATCHFUL	Look up antonyms of CARELESS.
WATERY	Look up WET.
WEAK	Look up antonyms of STRONG.
WEIRD	Look up QUEER.

WELL-NIGH	Look up ABOUT.
WENT	WENT is the past tense of GO.
WET	WET means covered with water or not yet <u>dry</u>. A *wet* road is usually slippery. *The park bench had a sign on it that said "Wet Paint."*

damp
moist
soggy
soaking
drenched
watery
rainy
sloppy

Damp and *moist* mean slightly wet. *Use a damp cloth to wipe away the fingerprints.* Your hair may feel *damp* after you take a shower or get caught in the rain. Just after a rainstorm the air feels *moist.*

Soggy means heavy with water or moisture. A swamp is *soggy,* but a desert is <u>arid</u> and <u>dry</u>.

Soaking and *drenched* mean completely wet. *I tried to squeeze the water out of my soaking shirt. Before we got out of the rain, we were completely drenched.*

Watery means containing water. *The soup didn't have much flavor; it was too watery.* Land so dried out that it contains no water is <u>parched</u>.

On a *rainy* afternoon you must play indoors or put on your raincoat and boots before going outside or to a friend's house.

Sloppy can mean wet enough to spatter and splash. When snow begins to melt, it becomes *sloppy.* Some sandwiches are called "Sloppy Joes" because they may splash when you eat them.

ANTONYMS: <u>arid</u>, <u>dry</u>, <u>parched</u>

sloppy

217

WHISPER	Look up antonyms of SHOUT.
WIDE	Look up antonyms of THIN.
WILD	Look up antonyms of QUIET (adj).
WIN	Look up GET.
WISE	Look up SMART (adj).
WITTY	Look up FUNNY.
WOEBEGONE	Look up SAD. Look up antonyms of HAPPY.
WON	WON is the past tense and past participle of WIN.
WONDER	Look up THINK.

woebegone

WONDERFUL

WONDERFUL is one of the weariest words in our language. Originally *wonderful* and wondrous meant full of wonder or surprise. Now most people use *wonderful* for anything that is the least bit pleasing, exciting, remarkable, or good. They read a *wonderful* book, meet a *wonderful* person, have a *wonderful* trip, see a *wonderful* movie, or eat a *wonderful* piece of apple pie.

pleasant
delightful
enjoyable
astonishing
marvelous
fabulous
splendid
superb
spectacular

How about trying some other *wonderful* words? If something gives pleasure or joy, it is *pleasant,* *delightful,* or *enjoyable.* *The puppet show was **delightful.*** *They spent a **pleasant** day. Tom had an **enjoyable** trip.* ***Astonishing, marvelous,*** *and **fabulous** mean beyond* believing. *The painting was so real it was **astonishing.*** *He has a **marvelous** voice. The stories he tells are **fabulous.*** ***Splendid*** *and **superb** mean unusually fine or* excellent. *The **splendid** carvings were on display at the* *museum. He did a **splendid** job of acting like an old man. We expected to see a good movie, but this one was **superb**.*

*__Spectacular__ means unusual, notable, or entertaining. The swimmer made a **spectacular** dive. The fireworks last night were truly **spectacular**.*

You will find some more ***wonderful*** words that you may be able to use if you look up BEAUTIFUL, BRAVE, BRIGHT, CLEAN, FUNNY, GOOD, GREAT, HAPPY, IMPORTANT, INTERESTING, KIND, RIGHT, SMART (adj).

ANTONYMS: <u>ordinary</u>, <u>plain</u>

work

WORK	Look up RUN.
WRECK	Look up BREAK. Look up antonyms of MAKE.
WRETCHED	Look up SAD. Look up antonyms of HAPPY.
WRINKLED	Look up antonyms of SMOOTH.
WRONG	Look up BAD. Look up antonyms of RIGHT.

219

YELL   Look up SAY and SHOUT.

YODEL   Look up SHOUT.

YOUNG   Look up antonyms of OLD.

yodel

3 Sets

When you think of a set of twins, you really picture two brothers or two sisters or a brother and sister. They were born at the same time, and perhaps they look so much alike that you can't tell them apart. When you think of a set of dishes, you picture a number of plates and cups and saucers all having the same color or pattern. You probably think about sets of numbers every day in math class.

A set is a collection of things. It may be things that belong together, like a set of twins, or things that are used together, like a set of dishes.

A set can be a group of things that grow together, like grapes or trees.

A set can be a family of animals that live together, like bees or sheep.

A set can be a group of people who work or play together or who are all interested in one thing, like Scouts or Little Leaguers.

A set can be things that are put together or held in different ways, like sticks or hay.

A set can be things to ride in or on.

In our language there are many special words that have the same meaning as *set*. But these words are not synonyms.

The following pages contain names for different kinds of sets.

THINGS

bunch

clump

cluster

bale

bundle

delta

isthmus ⟶

peninsula

island

atoll

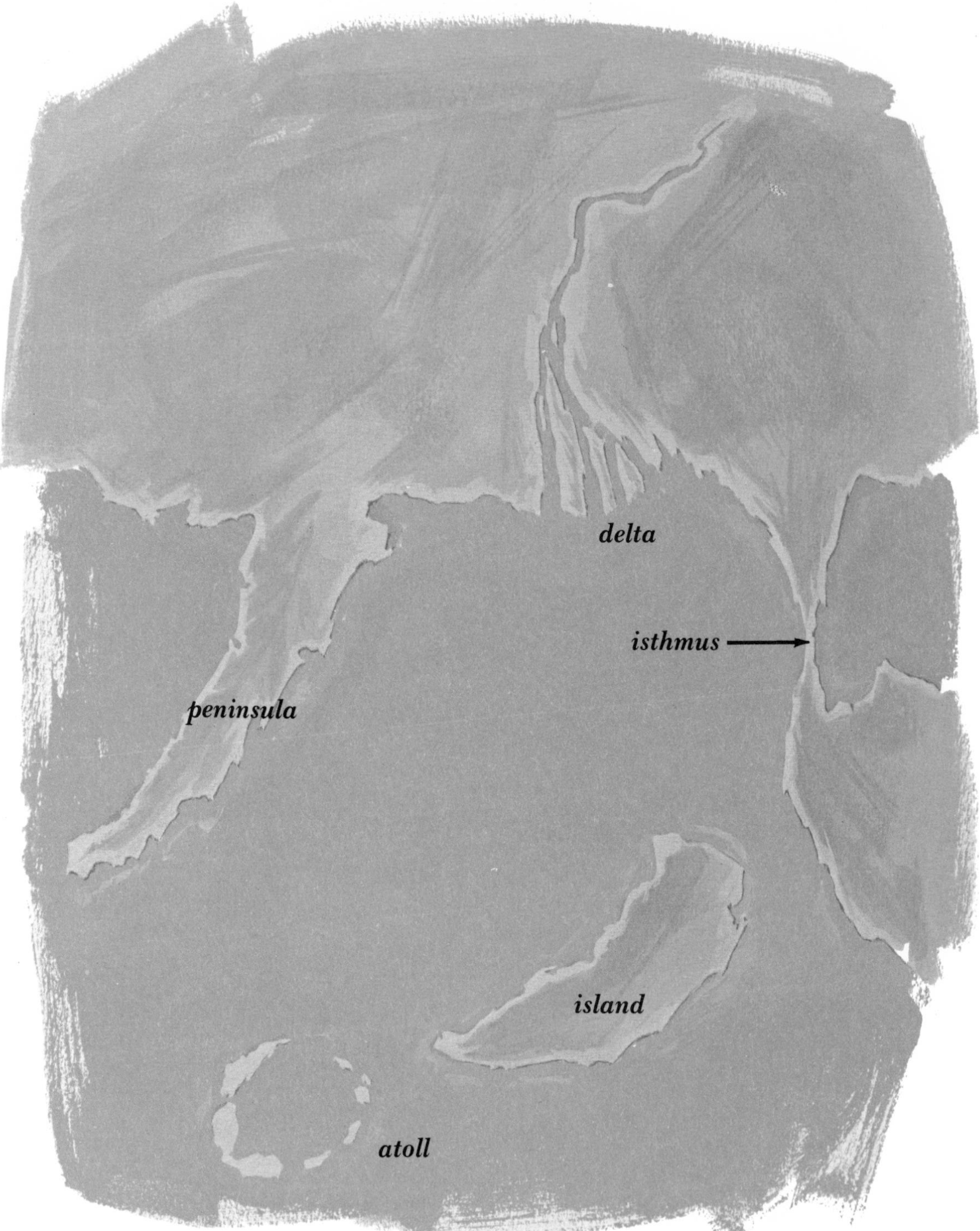

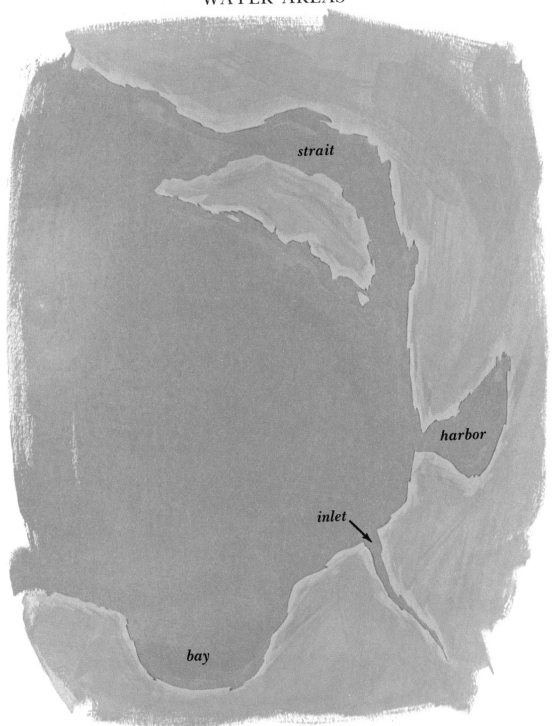

strait

harbor

inlet

bay

HIGH LAND

hill

knoll

mountain

mesa

butte

cliff

LOW LAND

valley

gorge

ravine

canyon

river

brook
creek

spring

rivulet

cataract

rapids

STILL WATER

lake

pond

swamp
marsh

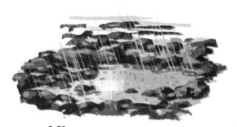

puddle

water hole

ANIMALS

pack

swarm

school

ANIMALS

litter

flock

herd

ANIMALS

skein of geese

brace of ducks

brood of chicks

pride of lions

ANIMALS

pod of seals

covey of quail

gaggle of geese

PEOPLE

congregation

audience

crowd

class

PEOPLE

troop of Brownies

team

squad

troupe of acrobats

TRAINS

caravan

safari

wagon train

freight train

convoy

WAYS TO RIDE

rickshaw

howdah

chariot

sedan chair

buggy

sleigh

dog sled

ski lift

BOATS

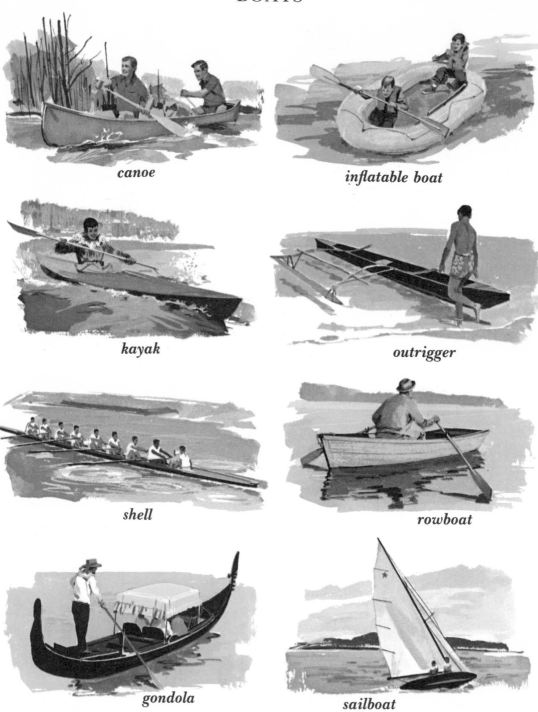

canoe

inflatable boat

kayak

outrigger

shell

rowboat

gondola

sailboat

SHIPS

Viking ship

Spanish galleon

Chinese junk

Yankee clipper

hydrofoil

stern-wheeler

ferry

barge

Acknowledgment is made for the following photographs:

Page 39, Camera Hawaii—Alpha / Page 42, Photo by Hiro Mizushima—Grant/Jacoby / Page 50, Photo by H. Armstrong Roberts / Page 85, Photos by Whittaker-Guernsey / Page 88, Photo by L. Willinger—FPG.

4 5 6 7 8 9 10 11 12 13 14 15 16 17 18 19 20 21 22 23 24 25   D   72 71 70

240